Quick and Easy
Knit & Crochet

Leslie Linsley

St. Martin's/Marek
New York

Quick and Easy Knit & Crochet

Preparation and design: Jon Aron Studio

Art direction:	Jon Aron
Research:	Amy Brunhuber
Illustrations:	Greg Worth
Photography:	Jon Aron
	Brad Stanton
Craft contributors:	Anna Beck
	Sally V. George
	Sylvia Kaplan
	Anne Lane
	Ruth Linsley
	Mrs. Murray
	Robin Marie Murray

Library of Congress Cataloging in Publication Data
Linsley, Leslie.
   Quick and easy knit & crochet
   1. Knitting.   2. Crocheting.   I. Title.
TT820.L69   1983   746.43   82–23076
ISBN 0-312-66047-2

First Edition
10 9 8 7 6 5 4 3 2 1

I am especially grateful to Robin Marie Murray for her technical and creative contributions throughout the production of this book.

I would like to thank Carol Peters at Creative Needles, New York City, for her invaluable input.

My appreciation is also extended to the yarn manufacturers and distributors who have been helpful in the preparation of this book. Their cooperation and interest in furnishing the beautiful materials for the purpose of designing the projects have been most generous. They are:

Bernat Yarn and Craft Corp., Uxbridge, Massachusetts
Bucilla, New York, New York
Coats & Clark, Inc., Stamford, Connecticut
Gemini innovations ltd., Huntington Station, New York
Laines Anny Blatt, Southfield, Michigan
Phildar, Inc., Norcross, Georgia
Tahki Imports Ltd., Hackensack, New Jersey

L.L.

Contents

Getting started in crochet   69

Crocheting tips   75

Crochet abbreviations   77

Source list

A section of color photographs follows page 128.

easy-to-knit child's sweater

Quick and Easy
Knit & Crochet

Introduction

When I began to think about a knit and crochet book, I thought it was because these crafting techniques had suddenly become more popular than ever before. Perhaps this is so, but everyone who knits and crochets will quickly tell you that these needlecrafts have always been second nature to their mothers, grandmothers, aunts or great-grandmothers, and that knitting and crocheting have always been popular and practical pastimes.

It's been my experience that all crafts come and go and come back into vogue again in regular cyclical patterns. And so my awareness of what appears to be a sudden interest in knitting and crocheting is due to its visibly increased popularity.

Designer sweaters are more beautiful than ever before, but they are extremely expensive. This is an incentive to make our own. With knowledge of a few basic stitches, you can easily create as nice a garment for less than one third the cost.

If you've never worked with yarn before, you are in for a treat. The materials that you'll be working with will bring out the creativity in the least creative. The first awareness that you are about to embark on a wonderful new experience comes about when you walk into the yarn shop. This is a good place to start, even before you know what you will make. The combination of colors and textures will stimulate your imagination. Who can resist the desire to make something in a favorite color? The variety of bulky yarns conjures up the image of a warm winter sweater, or the soft, fluffy mohairs of a delicate shawl; or perhaps it's the wonderful novelty yarns in multiple colors that will bring out your creative urges.

Once you decide to knit or crochet your first project, you'll find a whole new world opened to you. Whether it's an easy-to-make scarf, a child's simple cap or a designer-look sweater, the project can only be a satisfying experience, leading to more.

As you learn how to combine yarns, to use smaller or larger needles, to create different looks from varying patterns and yarns, you'll want to design your own projects. You'll see how easy it is to experiment with different stitches, substitute colors or make changes in a basic pattern for a one-of-a-kind project. For example, on page 32 you'll find a simple vest designed for a beginner to knit in a few hours. The vest is made in one color with an inexpensive sportyarn. The embroidered neckline was done by sewing over the original stitches, and this can be done in any design you might like to add. The vest is made in one piece, and can be adapted for any man's or child's size as well. It's a good basic pattern for a first project. If you want to make it more interesting, simply add a stripe or two using a contrasting color, and add a matching scarf. Now turn to page 34, and you'll find the identical pattern made exactly the same way with ribbon rather than yarn. Here we have a dressier top, with a flower at the neckline for added interest.

All of us have a lot less time these days for crafting, and even an experienced needleworker is not eager to take on a long and complicated project. In preparing this book I spoke to many long-time knitters and crocheters who expressed a desire for more quick and easy projects that didn't look uninteresting. Useful projects were more desirable than clothing. These included household accessories such as place mats, and trims for napkins, handkerchiefs and towels. People wanted to give gifts that had a handmade quality without spending hours to create them.

Carryalls and tote bags were of interest, as well as baby blankets and afghans. Many people expressed a desire to make a baby gift, but were reluctant to spend hours working with fine yarns that required small needles. The reason was that they felt the child would grow too fast to get much wear from the item. Therefore, we designed some projects that could be worked quickly on larger needles using bulkier yarn for a slightly different kind of look in baby wear. (See pages 48, 60 and 62.)

While I have been told by many experts in the field of knitting and crocheting, those who own yarn shops and manufacturers of the yarns, that within the year Americans will be following the European lead in the use of small needles, this book does not direct itself to such projects. Because we are concentrating on the quick and easy aspect of the crafts, almost all projects are done on needles from #6 up to #13. When we wanted a soft, delicate project using the finer yarns, in most cases we plied two or three strands together or combined it with a heavier yarn. A variety of colors was also employed to give a look of unexpected softness to bulky items.

Some of the crochet projects required the lacy look that can be achieved only with fine cotton thread and an equally fine crochet hook. In these cases the projects are small, so that the work is confined and the results are special. For these projects, however, there is an alternate version in the same pattern, only using a larger hook and heavier yarn, with directions on how to expand the project. For example, on page 98 you will find a lace doily made up of 37 medallions worked with #40 cotton thread (very fine) on a #14 steel hook that is almost as fine as a needle. If one were ambitious, this project could be expanded to become a full tablecloth. On page 96 you will find a pincushion

crocheting lace doily

crocheting medallion for pin cushion

project made from one of these medallions, done with a heavier crochet yarn and larger hook. This medallion is about 7 times larger than those in the doily, and it too can be expanded by making multiples for a larger project.

The patterns have all been carefully worked out so that once used one way, they can be adapted for other projects. In this way, if you make something and like the results, you can make it again with an entirely different look. The carryall on page 92 is one example of a brightly striped cotton crochet project perfect for summer toting. This can also be worked with more subdued colors; and by combining rust and navy cotton, for example, plied together, the maker gets an effect like that of a tweed bag. The materials for both are the same, only used differently. The directions are also the same. Therefore, once you are familiar with a pattern, it's fun to use it again in a whole new way. This is especially true in making a garment, since you can adjust it to fit the person who will wear it. When you make it again in another color combination or with other yarn, you're more familiar with what you are doing.

The stitches used in all these projects are basic. There are no fancy or complicated stitches. However, the projects have been designed to look best with traditional, easy-to-work stitches; for those who are more experienced, more intricate stitches can be applied. The book is intended as a jumping-off point. Once you've made some projects with the basic stitches and patterns provided, you may want to expand your interest in this area. And I think even the most experienced among you will find the projects varied and good-looking and, with their added element of speed and easiness, will find them both rewarding and enjoyable to make.

Getting started in knitting

Knitting is based on learning how to do two basic stitches, knit and purl. From these you can make all kinds of knitted projects. By combining these two stitches in different variations, such as 2 knit, 2 purl, or 1 row of knit and 1 row of purl, you will be able to create a simple garment or as elaborate a project as you can imagine.

As a beginner, you will find that most of the projects in this book confine themselves to a basic knit and purl stitch to produce what is known as a stockinette pattern. This is the most popular stitch combination, and is easy to learn. If you are a practiced knitter, you'll find a variety of projects that introduce new ideas and combinations of yarn that will make it enjoyable to do. Best of all, the projects are quick and easy, but the results should be rewardingly professional-looking.

The following will teach you what you need to know in order to make the knitting projects in this book. You will also be able to go on to create your own designs or variations on the original patterns.

Casting on

To begin any project, you will need to cast a specified number of stitches onto your needles. This becomes your base from which you will work your first row of knitting. When counting rows, do not count the cast-on row.

1. Start by making a slip knot, leaving a tail of yarn about 3 inches long. Place the loop of the knot on the left-hand needle. (For left-handers, reverse these and all other instructions.) Use your right-hand needle to make the stitches to cast onto the left-hand needle as follows.

2. Wrap the yarn around your left forefinger to create tension, and insert the right-hand needle from front to back through the loop on the left-hand needle. The two needles are now in the loop, with the right-hand needle behind the left.

3. Bring the yarn clockwise around the right-hand needle. With the right-hand needle, pull the yarn through the loop on the left needle.

4. Bring the tip of the left-hand needle from right to left through the loop on the right needle.

5. Withdraw the right-hand needle, pull the yarn slightly taut and you have 2 stitches on the left needle. Continue to do this until you have the number of stitches needed.

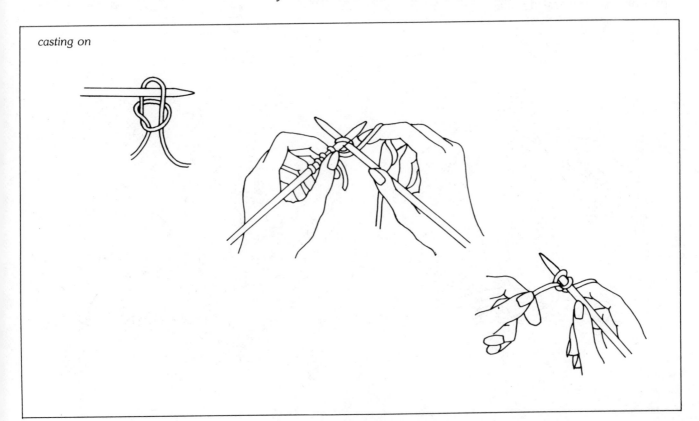

casting on

Knit stitch

A project worked with all knitting stitches is called a garter-stitch fabric.

1. Hold the needle with cast-on stitches in your left hand, with the yarn around your left forefinger. Insert the right-hand needle from front to back through the first loop on the left-hand needle.

2. Bring the yarn under and over the point of the right needle. Draw the yarn through the loop with the point of the needle.

3. Use your right forefinger to push the tip of the left needle down, to let the loop on the left needle slip off. You now have one stitch on your right needle. Work across the row in this way.

After finishing a row of knitting, transfer the right-hand needle to left hand and the left to the right, turning the needles also (the points always face each other), and continue the next row in the same way, always taking the stitches from the left to the right needle.

When you have practiced making nice neat rows at an even tension, you can turn this garter stitch into a project. Try the basic scarf on page 28 without the pockets (until you learn to purl and can add the details).

garter stitch fabric

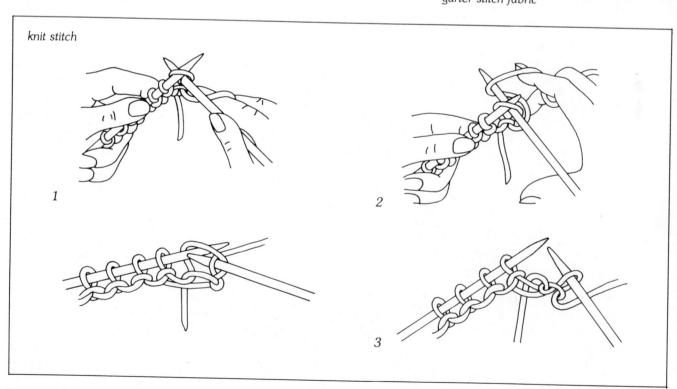

knit stitch

1

2

3

Purl stitch

1. With cast-on stitches on your left-hand needle, insert the point of your right-hand needle from right to left through the *front* of the first stitch. With the yarn in front of your work (rather than in back as with the knit stitch) wind it over and around the needle's point.

2. Draw the yarn back through the stitch and let the loop on the left needle slip off the needle. Your first purl stitch is now on your right-hand needle.

Stockinette stitch

Work one row with the knit stitch. Purl each stitch in the next row. Continue to knit one row and purl the next for a stockinette fabric. The pattern on the front of the work is that of interlocking V's. The back of the fabric looks like a tighter version of all garter stitch (knit).

stockinette stitch fabric

Increasing a stitch

This means that you will be making two stitches from one on a row. Knit the first stitch as usual, but do not drop the stitch off the left-hand needle. Bring the right-hand needle behind the left needle and insert it from right to left into the back of the same stitch. Make another stitch by winding yarn under and over the right-hand needle (knit stitch). Slip the stitch off the left-hand needle.

If you are increasing a stitch on a purl row, purl the first stitch but do not slip it off. Bring the yarn between the needles to the back of the work, and *knit* a stitch in back of the same stitch unless otherwise instructed.

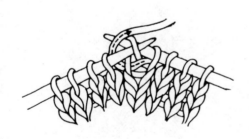

Decreasing a stitch

If you are decreasing stitches, to shape a raglan armhole for example, you will be knitting or purling two stitches together to form one stitch. In a pattern direction this will be given as K2 tog or P2 tog.

On the right side of your work, knit 2 stitches together as if they were one. If worked through the front of the stitches, the decrease slants to the right, if through the back of the stitches it slants to the left.

When decreasing a purl stitch, work on the wrong side and purl 2 stitches together.

Psso means pass slip stitch over, and is another way of decreasing a stitch. You slip the first stitch by taking it onto the right-hand needle from the left without knitting it, keeping the yarn in back of the work. Knit the next stitch and bring the slip stitch over the knit stitch as you would when binding off. (When slipping a stitch in a purl row, keep the yarn in front of the work.)

Binding off

1. Knit the first two stitches. Insert the left-hand needle from left to right through the front of the first (the right-most) stitch.
2. Lift the first stitch over the second stitch and the tip of the right-hand needle. (Use your left hand to push the tip of the right-hand needle back while pulling the stitch through.) Let the lifted stitch drop, and you now have one stitch on the right-hand needle. Knit another stitch and lift the right-most stitch over the next as before. Repeat this across the row until one stitch is left.
3. Loosen the remaining loop on the right-hand needle and withdraw the needle. Cut the yarn, leaving 2 or 3 inches (unless the instructions for your project specify a longer tail), and pull this tail through the loop. Tighten the knot.

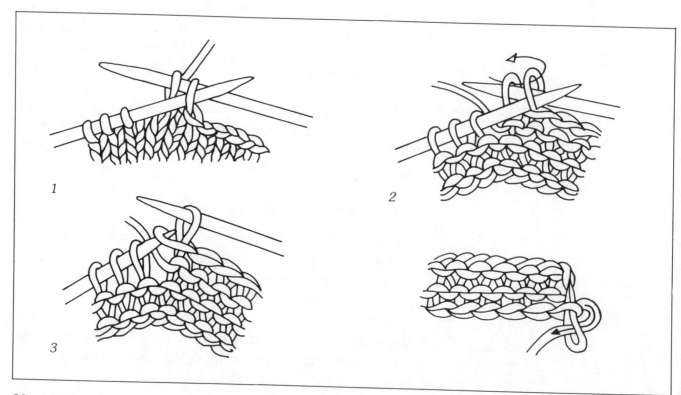

1

2

3

Cable stitches

Cable stitches are often used in fisherman-knit sweaters and add interest to a plain pullover such as the project on page 58.

Producing a cable twist requires the use of a double-pointed cable needle. This should be the same size or slightly smaller than those used to knit the garment.

Determine where the cable stitch will be and begin on the right side of the work. Purl across until you come to the point where the cable will begin. Using the cable needle, place one end from right to left through the next stitch. Allow this stitch to slip off the left-hand needle (reverse for left-handed people). Repeat for the next two stitches. With the three stitches on the cable needle, keep it at the front of the work. Ignoring this needle, take the yarn to the back of the work and knit the next three stitches with the other two needles as usual.

Next, hold the cable needle with your left hand and push the stitches to the right side of the needle. Using the right-hand needle and the cable needle, knit the three stitches on the cable needle. Purl to the end of the row. Work the straight rows between cable twists according to the directions for each project. Always twist your cable on the right side. The cable will have tighter or looser twists depending on the number of rows between twists. The fewer the rows between twists, the tighter the cable pattern.

Joining new yarn

Always join new yarn at the beginning of a row. If you get partway across and run out of yarn, pull out stitches to the beginning of the row and add the new yarn. (This is to avoid knots in the middle of a piece.) Insert the right-hand needle into the first stitch on the left-hand needle. Wrap the new yarn around the right-hand needle, leaving a tail as you did when starting your work. Pull the right-hand needle through the first stitch and continue to knit as before. Pull the side strands of yarn to tighten. Use these to attach pieces of the project being worked, or weave them into the project later.

Knitting tips

Yarn

There are hundreds of yarns to choose from, and each has its best uses. Most patterns recommend the best yarn for the project. If the brand name is not given, the yarn group usually is. This might be a bulky weight, worsted, sportyarn, etc. If you are substituting yarns for those given in a pattern, be sure that the weight is similar. Look for a yarn with the same gauge. This information is usually found on the label of the yarn.

Often the yarn looks quite different, when it is made up, from what it looked like on the skein. It's a good idea, especially when using expensive yarn or when making a large project, to buy only one skein and make a swatch. In this way you can see what the knitted yarn will look like before making the investment of time and money. Buy enough yarn needed for a project. Often colors change from one dye lot to another and you may have trouble matching yarns later on if you run out.

Gauge

The gauge is the number of stitches and number of rows per inch you knit with the yarn and needles recommended. The gauge is the tension at which you work, and this determines the size of the project. This is especially important when making a garment to wear. If your gauge doesn't match the gauge given with the pattern, the garment won't fit as stated.

Before beginning any project, test your gauge by making a swatch using the yarn and needles recommended. Knit in the stitch pattern for a 4 × 4-inch square. Check the gauge given and mark the number of stitches with pins. For example, if the gauge calls for 7 stitches to 2 inches, count 7 stitches in the middle of the work and mark where they begin and end. With a tape measure check to see what the measurement is for 7 stitches. If the 7 stitches makes less than 2 inches, your gauge is too tight. Make another sample with needles a size larger. If the 7 stitches measures more than 2 inches, you will need to go down a size with your needles. Sometimes the gauge difference occurs because the yarn used is not exactly what is recommended in the directions.

count rows per inch for gauge

count stitches per inch for gauge

Blocking

When making a garment, it's important to block each piece after it is finished. This will make it easier to put the pieces together and it will fit better.

Different yarns are treated differently, and this is why it's important to keep the labels from your yarn to refer to after the knitting has been completed. Sometimes the label gives blocking directions, but if not, you will need the information concerning what the yarn is made of.

When making a sweater, for example, you want each piece to have the correct shape. If you've worked in a stockinette stitch, the edges tend to curl and blocking is necessary. Each piece must be pinned down and pressed. The iron setting depends on the yarn. Use a cool iron on synthetic material, but natural fibers can be pressed with a warm iron. Some blocking is done by placing a damp cloth over the shaped and pinned piece. Wait until the piece is dry before removing the pins. It is not advisable to press over a garter stitch (all knit).

Assembling pieces

There are many ways to assemble the pieces of a garment or other project that must be stitched together. Some patterns here recommend leaving enough of a tail of the yarn being used to sew pieces together. In this way you have the yarn in place for the pieces and everything matches.

Main seams on shoulders, at sides or on sleeves are usually joined with a backstitch. Use a blunt yarn needle, and with right sides of fabric together make small stitches across the material just below the finished edges.

To join sections of ribbing use an overcast stitch. With right sides together and edges matching, overcast the yarn on both pieces. Do not pull the yarn too taut. This will give you a flat seam.

Another way to join seams, especially for bulky yarn, is with a slip stitch crochet. (See crochet how-to's on page 74.)

Setting in sleeves

Place the sleeve seam at the center of the underarm, with the center of the sleeve cap at the shoulder seam. Ease in any extra fullness all around so it is evenly curved. Join with the backstitch.

Knitting abbreviations

k—knit
p—purl
st—stitch
sts—stitches
sl—slip
sl st—slip stitch
yo—yarn over needle
sk—skip
rnd—round
tog—together
psso—pass slip stitch over
wyib—with yarn in back
wyif—with yarn in front
inc—increase
dec—decrease
rem—remaining
beg—beginning
pat—pattern
lp—loop
MC—main color
CC—contrasting color
dp—double-pointed needles
LH—left-hand needle
RH—right-hand needle

A simple blouson sweater

This short blouson sweater is an easy beginner's project, as it is made from four basic squares done on large-size needles. It can be worn over a shirt with the sleeves rolled up, or as is. It is easy to change the design for your needs by making the sleeves shorter or longer, and if you prefer, leave out the elastic from the waist and extend the length.

This sweater can be made in a variety of yarns, but if you use one with texture, as shown here, it will add interest to a very basic design.

The directions are given for a small (32), 17 inches across. Directions for medium (36), 19 inches across, and large (40), 21 inches across, are in parentheses.

Materials: Boucl' Anny from Anny Blatt—6 (7) (8) skeins Glacier color; ¼-inch elastic to fit waist.
Needles: #10
Gauge: 2½ stitches = 1 inch
        3 rows = 1 inch

Directions

Back: Cast on 44 (48) (52) sts. Knit entire piece in garter stitch (all knit).

Work the 44 sts until you have 12 (13) (14) inches—you are at the underarms. Mark at each end of work for armhole.

Continue knitting in garter stitch until you have 7 (7½) (8) inches from armhole markings. Entire piece should measure 19 (20½) (22) inches.

Bind off loosely.

Front: Repeat as for back.

Sleeves: Make 2. For each, cast on 36 (38) (40) sts. Knit in garter stitch (all knit) until piece measures 12 (13) (14) inches.

Bind off loosely.

Finish: Sew front and back together at shoulders with a 4 (4½) (5)-inch seam on each side. (See page 23 for assembling pieces.)

Sew sleeves from armhole markers on front to armhole markers on back. Sew each sleeve seam and side seam.

Run elastic through bottom edge to ease fullness and create blouson effect.

Christmas scarf

Make a surprise gift for your favorite child. The basic scarf is done entirely in the garter stitch (all knit), but it is the pockets that make it special. Each is made to look like a package, and inside each can be a present of finger puppets.

This is also an excellent project for a young child to learn knitting with. You might want to make a striped scarf of leftover yarns.

Materials: Wonderknit (Bucilla) yarn—3 skeins red, 1 skein green, 1 skein white.
Needles: #8
Gauge: 9 sts = 2 inches
       13 rows = 2 inches

Directions

With red, cast on 45 sts. Knit (garter stitch) entire piece 4 feet long. Bind off.

Pocket

Make 2. With white, cast on 40 sts for each. Knit in stockinette st (knit 1 row, purl 1 row) for 4 inches. End on wrong side (that is, with a purl row).

Change to green yarn. Knit all (garter stitch) for 6 rows.

Change to white and return to stockinette st for 4 inches. Bind off loosely.

Cast on 90 stitches in green yarn. Knit for 6 rows. Bind off loosely.

Make a bow in the center of the long green strip. Attach this vertical strip over horizontal stripe on pocket.

Turn side and bottom edges of pocket to underside and sew to one end of scarf. It should be placed approximately 1½ inches from bottom of scarf, so there is a red border all around pocket. Attach second pocket to other end of scarf, on same side.

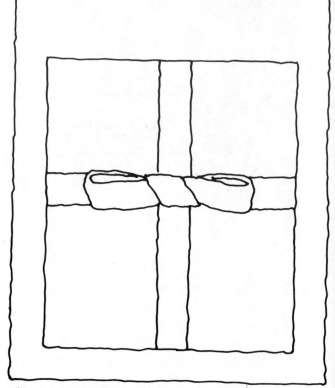

placement of pocket on scarf

Child's sport sweater

This is an easy sweater that even a child can learn to knit with a little help. The basic stockinette stitch (knit 1 row, purl 1 row) is used to create the four square pieces. Instructions are provided for a small size (4–6), with numbers in parentheses for medium size (8–10) and large size (12–14). You might consider making a matching sweater for a parent. This sweater is made in indigo blue, with a touch of off white in the detailing.

Materials: Bucilla St. Moritz sportyarn—2 (3) (3) skeins indigo blue, 1 skein oatmeal.
Needles: #11
Gauge: 3 sts = 1 inch
4 rows = 1 inch

Directions

Knit entire sweater in stockinette (k 1 row, p 1 row).

Back: With blue, cast on 38 (42) (46) sts and work first 2 inches. Then do 2 rows in oatmeal color (see page 21 for joining new yarn). Continue to work with blue color until entire piece measures 9½ (11) (12½) inches, or desired length from bottom edge to armhole.

Mark armhole edge by working next 2 rows in oatmeal color. Work 1 inch in blue, followed by 2 rows of oatmeal again.

Finish with 3 (3½) (4) inches of blue. Bind off loosely.

Front: Create front of sweater exactly as you did the back. Sew front and back together at shoulders with 3 (3¼) (3½)-inch seams from each shoulder edge to neck opening. (See page 23 for assembling pieces.)

Sleeves: Pick up 28 (32) (36) sts from armhole-edge stripe on front piece to armhole-edge stripe on back piece. With blue, work 2 inches, then stripe sequence (2 rows oatmeal, 1 inch blue, 2 rows oatmeal). Continue blue color for 6 (6½) (8) inches. Then continue with 2 rows oatmeal, then 2 inches blue.

Bind off. Repeat for other sleeve. Sew side seams and sleeves.

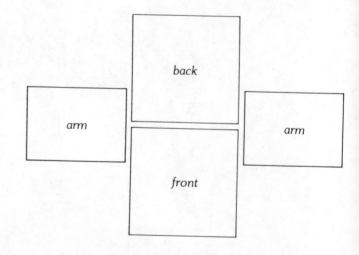

Versatile vest

This vest can be made in a variety of ways and is a good first project. The sportyarn used here creates a bulky, everyday warm garment. The same pattern can be used to create an evening top made from metallic yarns, ribbon (see page 34) or soft angora.

It has been designed to be worn by a man or woman, or, if made smaller, by a child. If you'd like to make an outfit, add a scarf with contrasting stripes (another easy beginner). For interest you can add a ruffled collar or consider a stripe in another color. You can leave this vest as is, or add an embroidered design to the color (see chart for placement). The crocheted hat on page 000 can also be made to match. Directions given for small (M) (L) size.

Materials: Bucilla St. Moritz sportyarn—3 3½-oz. skeins, berry color.
Needles: #11
Gauge: 12 sts, 16 rows = 4 inches

Pattern: The entire project is worked in ribbing (k 1 st, p 1 st).

Directions

Cast on 50 (54) (58) sts. Work pattern for 10 (11) (12) inches. Mark for armhole edge. Work across row 23 (25) (27) sts. Knit next 2 sts together.

Attach second skein of yarn. Knit first 2 sts tog and continue across row in pattern. Continue working both sides equally until distance (from knit 2 tog and attached second ball of yarn) is 15 (16) (17) inches.

Joining row: Work across first half. Inc 1 st at end of first half and 1 at beg of 2nd half, joining halves tog by using the first skein only.

Mark for armholes on outside edges. Continue working in pattern until the length from armhole is 10 (11) (12) inches. Bind off evenly.

Finish: Sew side seams from bottom to armhole edge markings.

Embroidery: Embroidery is added over original knitted stitches. Select yarn colors in similar weight as vest. Thread large-eye needle with yarn. Do not knot yarn. Begin from wrong side and weave an inch of yarn under a couple of stitches.

Bring needle through to right side of work at base of first stitch to be covered. Insert needle from right to left under vertical loops of stitch in the row above. Insert needle into base of stitch you are covering. Do not pull the yarn taut, as it should be kept at gauge of yarn you are covering.

When finishing off a color, weave end of yarn under a couple of stitches on wrong side of work. Follow chart for placement of design.

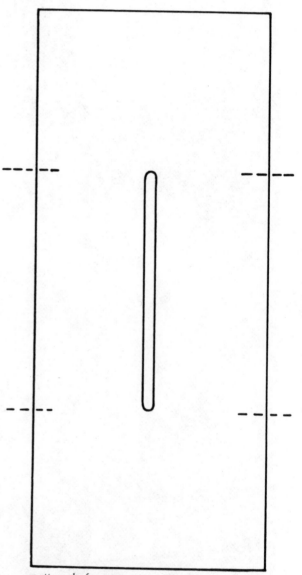

pattern before joining side seams

Ribbon top

The pattern for this evening or summer sweater is identical to that used to make the vest on page 32 but is knitted with rayon ribbon. Made in one piece, it is an extremely quick and easy project, yet looks quite beautiful. Wear it as is or over a silky blouse. The crocheted flower is added for detail and is made with the same ribbon.

This project is made in one color, but you might try making it multicolored by using, for example, two or three stripes at the waist.

Materials: Gemini rayon ribbon—3 rolls ½-inch-wide, ecru color.
Needles: #11; crochet hook for flower #K
Gauge: Same as page 32.

Directions

(See pages 69–77 for crocheting instructions and abbreviations to make flower decoration.)

Vest: Follow instructions on page 32.

Flower: Ch 6 for center layer. Join with sl st to form a ring.

Rnd 1: Ch 2, 2 tr, 1 dc in the same st (as the sl st), 1 sc in next ch. * 1 dc, 2 tr, 1 dc in the next ch, 1 sc in the next ch, repeat from * around, end off. You have created a large flower to which you will attach a smaller flower. Proceed as follows.

Next layer: Ch 10, join with sl st, repeat rnd 1. To form flower, join 2 layers with sl st.

Leaves (if desired): Join contrasting color with sl st in a corner of outer layer of flower, ch 4, 1 dc in same space, ch 4. Join with sl st in same corner st. Repeat for 2 more leaves.

Mouse slippers

The body of each of these little mouse slippers is knit, while the ears are made with simple crochet. If you prefer to knit the entire project, see page 152 for knitting instructions for ears. If you do this, stitch pink felt to front of gray knit ears. The face is embroidered last.

The slippers are made to fit a 2–4-year-old child; however, directions for the next two larger sizes are indicated in parentheses.

Materials: 4-oz. ball gray worsted, scrap of pink worsted (Bucilla), 2 buttons for eyes.
Needles: #10, crochet hook #7
Gauge: 4 sts = 1 inch
      6 rows (3 garter stitch ridges) = 1 inch

Directions

For this project we used a double strand of worsted on #10 needles. However, you can substitute one strand of bulky yarn if desired.

Cast on 29 (35) (41) sts.
Row 1: Knit.
Row 2: K 9 (11) (13), * p 1, k 9 (11) (13), repeat from * once more. Repeat rows 1 and 2 until there are 13 (16) (19) garter stitch ridges on right side, ending with row 2.

Shape Toe

Row 1: P 1, * k 1, p 1, repeat from * across row.
Row 2: K 1, * p 1, k 1, repeat from * across row. Repeat these 2 rows 3 (5) (7) times more, then work row 1 once more.

Break off yarn, leaving an 8-inch end.

Finish: Draw end through remaining sts and pull up tightly. Sew ribbing edges together to form toe. Fold the cast-on edge in half and seam for center back. (See page 152 for crochet instructions to make ears.)

Ears

Make 4. With pink yarn, ch 6; sc on 2nd ch from hook, and 4 sc across row. Sc 1, turn work and sc 4 across. Repeat 3 times (see diagram).

Ch 1, turn work and * insert hook into next sc, yo, pull lp through, repeat from * 3 times (5 lps on hook);

yo, pull through all 5 lps. Ch 1.
Fasten off.
Attach gray yarn at beg corner first sc.
Working up the ear (ch 2, 1 dc) 4 times, (1 hdc, 1 sc) into top loop, ch 1, turn.
(1 hdc, 5 dc) down. Ch 2, turn.
(4 dc back, 1 hdc, 1 sc) in top, (1 hdc, 4 dc) around other side of pink. (See diagram.)
Return with (ch 2, 4 dc, 1 hdc, 1 sc), ch 1.
Turn work and sc rows 3 and 5 to join ear.

Finish: Stitch ears in place on slipper using the gray yarn. Use 3 strands of gray yarn 4 inches long for whiskers. Thread each strand through from one side of toe front to the other so there are approximately 2 inches on either side of toe front. Attach movable or button eyes.

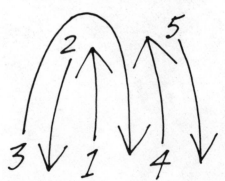

mouse ear sequence

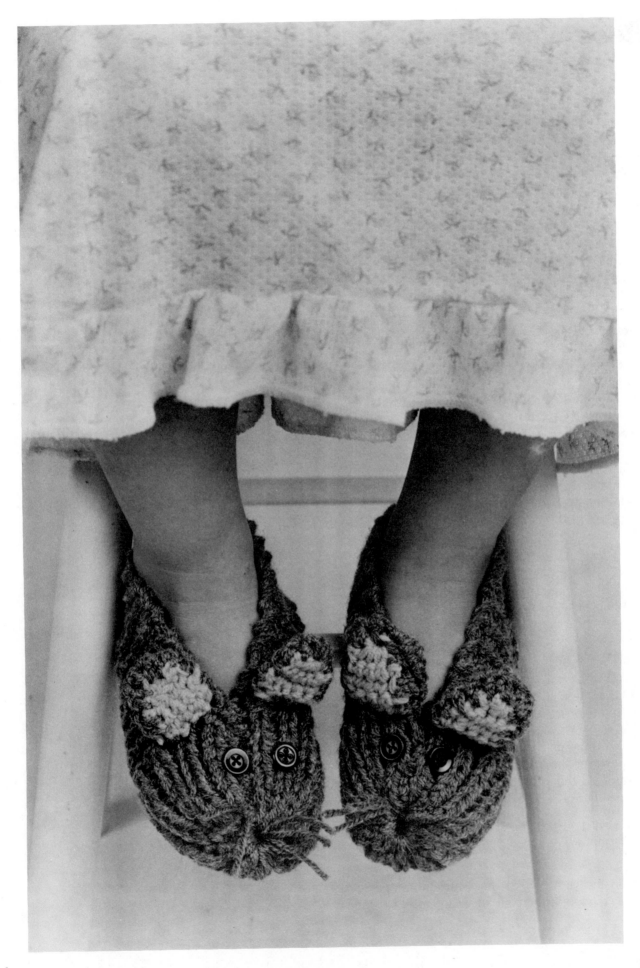

Rose slippers

These easy-knit slippers can be made to fit any size foot, and the decoration on the front can be changed depending on the person who will wear them. For example, these have a simple crocheted flower on each. If you make them for a child, you could knit or crochet bunny ears and add an embroidered face, with a pompom tail at the back, to each. Or you could simply make fat pompoms from scrap yarn to go on the front. This is a good last-minute gift to make from leftover yarn. The slippers can even be made from multicolored scraps.

Materials: 1 skein gray worsted yarn, small amount of pink worsted for roses.
Needles: #10, crochet hook #7
Gauge: 4 sts = 1 inch
6 rows (3 garter st ridges) = 1 inch

Directions

Make 2. The slippers will fit a child or up to size 6 woman's foot. Measurements for larger women's and for men's sizes are given in parentheses.

Cast on 35 (41) (47) sts in double worsted gray yarn.
Row : Knit.
Row 2: K 11 (13) (15), * p 1, k 11 (13) (15), repeat from * once more. Repeat rows 1 and 2 until there are 16 (19) (22) ridges on right side, ending with row 2.

Toe
Row 1: P 1, * k 1, p 1, repeat from * across row.
Row 2: K 1, * p 1, k 1, repeat from * across row.

Repeat these 2 rows 5 (7) (9) times more, then work row 1 once more. Break off yarn, leaving an 8-inch end.
Finish: Draw end through remaining sts and pull tightly. Form the toe by sewing ribbing edges together. Fold the cast-on edge in half and seam for center of back of slipper.

Rose (See pages 69–77 for crochet directions and abbreviations.)

Make 2.
Wind the yarn 3 or 4 times around your finger, remove the loop from your finger and fasten with a sl st.

Rnd 1: Ch 1, sc 17 in ring, sl st to first ch.
Rnd 2: Ch 6, skip 2 sc, 1 hdc into next sc, * ch 4, skip 2 sc, 1 hdc into next sc. Repeat from * 3 times more. Ch 4, sl st into 2nd of first ch 4.
Rnd 3: In each ch 4 sp, work (1 sc, 1 hdc, 3 dc, 1 hdc, 1 sc). End with sl st into first sc.
Rnd 4: Sl st into back of hdc on rnd 2. * Ch 5; keeping yarn at back of work, 1 sl st into back of next hdc on rnd 2, repeat from * 4 times more. Ch 5, sl st in same hdc as first sl st.
Rnd 5: In each ch 5 lp work (1 sc, 1 hdc, 5 dc, 1 sc), end with a sl st in first sc.
Rnd 6: Sl st in back of sl st on rnd 4. * Ch 6; keeping yarn at back of work, 1 sl st into next sl st on rnd 4. Repeat from * to end.
Rnd 7: In each ch 6 sp, work (1 sc, 1 hdc, 7 dc, 1 hdc, 1 sc), end with a sl st into first sc.

Fasten off. Leave enough yarn to sew flowers to the front of each slipper.

Doggy mittens

What little child wouldn't love to wear these puppy-dog mittens complete with floppy ears? They are easy to make, so you might consider this project for your next Christmas bazaar. Make several in different sizes and colors.

Materials: Bucilla Wonderknit yarn—2-oz. ball yellow; scrap of brown yarn of equal weight; 4 brown buttons for eyes.
Needles: #4 and #6
Gauge: 5 sts = 1 inch
  7 rows = 1 inch

Directions

Right mitten

Using #4 needles, cast on 30 (36) (40) sts. K 1, p 1 in ribbing for 2 (2) (2½) inches. Change to #6 needles and work in stockinette st (k 1 row, p 1 row) for 4 (4) (6) rows.

Shape thumb gusset
Row 1: K 14 (17) (19) sts, put a marker on the needle, inc 1 st in each of next 2 sts, put a marker on needle, k 14 (17) (19) sts.
Row 2 and all even rows: Purl. Be sure to slip the markers onto the right needle each time you come to them.
Row 3: K to first marker, inc 1 st in next st, k to 1 st before 2nd marker, inc 1 st in next st, k to end of row. Repeat rows 2 and 3 until there are 8 (10) (12) sts between markers, ending with a p row.
Row 7 (9) (11): K to first marker, sl these knitted 14 (17) (19) sts onto a holder, k to next marker, turn, sl remaining 14 (17) (19) sts onto another holder.

Thumb: Working on 8 (10) (12) sts, at beg of each of next 2 rows cast on 1 st. Work even rows in stockinette st on 10 (12) (14) sts until piece measures desired finished length, ending with a p row.
Shape top: K 2 tog across row. Break off yarn, leaving a 12-inch end. Pull end through 5 (6) (7) sts and draw up tightly. Sew seam.

Hand: Sl 14 (17) (19) sts onto larger needles (#6), join yarn at start of thumb and pick up 2 sts over thumb, k 14 (17) (19) sts from second holder onto same needle. Work even in stockinette st on 30 (36)

(40) sts until piece measures 1½ inches less than desired finished length, ending with a p row.

Shape top
Row 1: *K 2 tog, k 4 (4) (6) sts, repeat from * to end of row.
Row 2 and all even rows: Purl.
Row 3: *K 2 tog, K 3 (3) (5) sts, repeat from * to end of row. Continue in this manner to dec 5 (6) (5) sts every other row until 5 (6) (5) sts remain. Break off yarn, leaving a 12-inch end. Finish in same way as top of thumb.

Left Mitten

Work same as right mitten.

Ears

Make 4. Cast on 14 sts. Work 10 rows in stockinette st (k 1 row, p 1 row).
Next row: K 2 tog, k 3, k 2 tog, k 2 tog, k 3, k 2 tog.
Next row: Purl.
Next row: K 2 tog, k 1, k 2 tog, k 2 tog, k 1, k 2 tog.

Break off yarn, leaving an 8-inch end. Pull end through sts and draw up tightly. Sew seam.

Place in position on front of each mitten and stitch together.

Follow diagram for placement of button eyes and embroidered face.

Owl potholder

What to do with scraps of yarn? Make up a batch of knitted potholders to give as gifts or to sell at your next fund-raising event. They can be made in one color or a combination of colors, and if you use left-overs they won't cost you anything.

Materials: Acrylic knitting worsted, 2 buttons for owl eyes.
Needles: #6 or #7; dp needles

Directions

Front
   Cast on 30 sts. Work 4 rows in garter st (all knit).
Row 5: (right side) Knit.
Row 6: K 3, p 24, k 3.
Row 7 through 10: Repeat rows 5 and 6.
Row 11: K 8, p 14, k 8.
Row 12: K 3, p 5, k 14, p 5, k 3.
Row 13: K 8, p 3, k 8, p 3, k 8.
Row 14: K 3, p 5, k 3, p 8, k 3, p 5, k 3.
Row 15: K 8, p 3, sl next 2 sts on dp needle, hold in back of work. K next 2 sts, k 2 sts from dp needle, sl next 2 sts on dp needle, hold in front of work. K next 2 sts, k 2 sts from dp needle. P 3, k 8.
Rows 16 through 24: Repeat rows 14 and 13 four times, then repeat row 14.
Row 25: Repeat row 15.
Row 26 through 28: Repeat rows 14, 13, then 14 again.
Row 29: Repeat row 15.
Row 30: Repeat row 14.
Row 31 and 32: Repeat rows 11 and 12.
Rows 33 through 38: Repeat rows 5 and 6 three times.
Rows 39 through 43: Knit, bind off.

Back
   Cast on 22 sts. Work in stockinette st (k 1 row, p 1 row) for 32 rows. Bind off.

Finish: Sew back to center of back of the front with wrong sides together. This will add padding to center with single thickness around the border. Sew on buttons for eyes and embroider nose and feet with contrasting thread.

Rolled cap with crocheted rose

The rolled cap is a popular design because it looks good on everyone and it's easy to make. All garter stitch, the cap is wonderful in several colors as well as solid. This one is bright blue, and the addition of our crocheted rose gives it a one-of-a-kind personality.

Materials: Phildar Pegase #206—1 skein blue, 1 skein pink (or small amount for the rose).
Needles: #8; #7 crochet hook
Gauge: 4 sts = 1 inch
            8 rows = 1 inch

Directions

Cast on 70 sts. Work all garter stitch (k each row) for 9 inches.
Next row: * K 2 tog, k 5. Repeat from * across.
Next row: K entire row.
Next row: * K 2, k 2 tog. Repeat from * across.
Next row: All k.
Next row: K 2 tog across, ending with k 1. There will be 23 rem sts. Fasten off, leaving a long tail. Draw end through remaining sts. Pull tight. Fasten on wrong side. Sew seam.

Rose (See pages 69–77 for crochet directions and abbreviations.)

Directions

Wind the yarn 4 times about your finger, remove loop and fasten with a sl st.
Rnd 1: Ch 1, 17 sc in ring, sl st to first ch.
Rnd 2: Ch 6, skip 2 sc, 1 hdc into next sc, * ch 4, skip 2 sc, 1 hdc in next sc. Repeat from * 3 times more. Ch 4, sl st into 2nd of first ch 4.
Rnd 3: In each ch 4 sp, work (1 sc, 1 hdc, 3 dc, 1 hdc, 1 sc). End with sl st into first sc.
Rnd 4: Sl st into back of hdc on rnd 2. * Ch 5; keeping yarn at back of work, 1 sl st into back of next hdc on rnd 2, repeat from * 4 times more. Ch 5, sl st in same hdc as first sl st.
Rnd 5: In each ch-5 loop work (1 sc, 1 hdc, 5 dc, 1 hdc, 1 sc), end with sl st in first sc.
Rnd 6: Sl st in back of sl st on rnd 4. * Ch 6; keeping yarn at back of work, 1 sl st into next sl st on rnd 4. Repeat from * to end.
Rnd 7: In each ch-6 sp, work (1 sc, 1 hdc, 7 dc, 1 hdc,

1 sc), end with a sl st into first sc.
Fasten off. Leave enough yarn to sew to cap.

Finish:
Roll brim of cap back to desired position and pin rose to one side of cap above brim. Stitch into position with yarn ends from rose so center is attached and petals stand free.

Pastel ribbon sweater

This striped sweater is made with pastel ice-cream-colored rayon ribbon. It has a lustrous sheen resembling fine silk ribbon, and comes in ¼-inch and ½-inch widths. Because it can be made on #11 needles, this sweater can be completed in a weekend and is relatively inexpensive.

This sweater, designed by Robin Murray, shows how well the colors work together. However, in order to cut down on the cost of having to use several spools of ribbon, you might consider making this project in only two contrasting colors, alternating them.

Materials: 1 roll each of Gemini ½-inch ribbons in the following colors: A. dusty rose, B. seafoam green, C. white, D. pale pink, E. powder blue, F. lilac.
Needles: #11
Gauge: 3 sts = 1 inch
4 rows = 1 inch

Directions

The pattern is for a small size. Directions for medium and large sizes are indicated in parentheses.

Back

Cast on 46 (50) (54) sts in color A.
Color A: Work 5 rows in garter stitch (all knit).
Color B: P 1 row, k 1 row, p 1 row, k 1 row, p 1 row, k 1 row (6 rows stockinette).
Color C: K 1 row.
Color D: K 1 row, p 1 row, k 1 row, p 1 row, k 1 row (5 rows).
Color E: K 1 row, p 1 row (2 rows).
Color F: P 1 row, k 1 row, p 1 row, k 1 row, p 1 row, k 1 row, p 1 row, p 1 row (8 rows).
Color A: P 1 row, k 1 row (2 rows).
Color E: P 1 row, k 1 row, p 1 row, k 1 row, p 1 row, k 1 row (6 rows).
Color C: K 1 row.
Color B: K 1 row, p 1 row, k 1 row, p 1 row, k 1 row, p 1 row, k 1 row, p 1 row (8 rows).
Color F: P 1 row, p 1 row, k 1 row, p 1 row, k 1 row (5 rows).
Color D: K 2 rows.
Color A: P 1 row, k 1 row, p 1 row, k 1 row, p 1 row, k 1 row, p 1 row, k 1 row (8 rows).
Mark for armhole at each end of work.

Color E: K 1 row, p 1 row, k 1 row, p 1 row, k 1 row (5 rows).
Color C: P 1 row, k 1 row (2 rows).
Color D: Beginning with a k row, work stockinette st (k 1 row, p 1 row) for 10 rows.
Color F: P 1 row, k 1 row (2 rows).
Color B: Beginning with a k row, work stockinette st for 6 rows.
Color A: Work 4 rows in garter st (all k).
Bind off loosely.

Front
Same as back.

Sew shoulder seams—3 (3½) (3½) inches.
Sleeves
Each sleeve pattern is the same, but done with different colors.
Sleeve 1: Cast on 22 (24) (26) sts with color C. Work 4 rows all k. Change to color E. Work in stockinette st (k 1 row, p 1 row), increasing one st at each edge every 2 inches. Continue working color E until sleeve equals 16 (15½) (17) inches. Change to color F and work 6 rows all knit. Bind off loosely.

Sleeve 2: Use colors D, B, F.

With complete sweater opened up and lying flat, sew sleeves in place from marked edge of front armhole to back. Sew side and sleeve seams together last.

Soft cuddly baby blanket

The combination of a soft fluffy yarn and pastel colors makes a perfect carriage or crib blanket for a new baby. The material used here is Phildar's Vizir, which is a combination of mostly mohair and wool with a little acrylic. When brushed slightly, it fluffs up and gets full. Worked on large needles, the loose, lacy stitches add to the delicate nature of this project. Finished blanket without fringe measures 32 × 32 inches.

Materials: Phildar Vizir—3 skeins each of pink (Ibis #47), lavender (Violine #98), and light blue (Mesange #57).
Needles: #11
Gauge: 2½ sts = 1 inch

Directions

Cast on 72 sts.

Pattern I: You will be working 16 rows in lavender.
Row 1: K 4, p 4 across.
Row 2: P 4, k 4 across.
Rows 3 and 4: Repeat rows 1 and 2.
Rows 5 through 8: Repeat rows 2 and 1 twice.
Rows 9 through 12: Same as 1 through 4.
Rows 13 through 16: Same as 5 through 8. (On last row of pattern I, inc 1 stitch.)

Pattern II: You will be working 13 rows in pink on 73 stitches.
Row 1 and all odd rows (wrong side and all other wrong-side rows): Purl across.
Rows 2, 4, and 6: K 1, * yo, sl 1, k 1, psso, k 1, k 2 tog, yo, k 1. Repeat from * to end of row.
Row 8: K 2, * yo, sl 1, k 2 tog, psso, yo, k 3. Repeat from * to end of row, except end last repeat k 2.
Row 10: K 1, * k 2 tog, yo, k 1, yo, sl 1, k 1, psso, k 1. Repeat from * to end of row.
Row 12: K 2 tog, * yo, k 3, yo, sl 1, k 2 tog, psso. Repeat from * another ten times; end yo, k 3, yo, sl 1, k 1, psso.
Row 13: Repeat Row 1. Decrease last row 1 st by knitting 2 tog (72 stitches).

Pattern III: You will be working 15 rows in blue.
Row 1: * P 3, k 3, repeat from * across row.

Row 2 and all other even-numbered rows: K all p sts in previous row and p all k sts.
Row 3: P 2, * k 3, p 3. Repeat from * ten more times; end k 3, p 2.
Row 5: P 1, * k 3, p 3. Repeat from * ten more times; end k 3, p 2.
Row 7: * K 3, p 3. Repeat from *
Row 9: K 2, * p 3, k 3. Repeat from * ten more times; end p 3, k 1.
Row 11: K 1, * p 3, k 3. Repeat from * ten more times; end p 3, k 2.
Row 12: same as row 2.
Repeat rows 1 through 3. On last row inc 1 st.

Color and pattern sequence
Pattern I: Lavender, 16 rows
Pattern II: Pink, 13 rows
Pattern III: Blue, 15 rows
Pattern II: Pink, 13 rows
Pattern I: Lavender, 16 rows
Pattern II: Pink, 13 rows
Pattern III: Blue, 15 rows
Pattern II: Pink, 13 rows
Pattern I: Lavender, 16 rows

Bind off loosely.
If you want to finish the ends with fringe, use the 3 colors of yarn together and, working with 3-inch lengths, knot fringe evenly along the 2 end edges.
Ribbons (optional). Weave ½-inch satin ribbon even spaced through open work of pattern.

Guest towel with seashore edging

A knitted edging can be as lovely as those done in crochet (see pages 106–109). When selecting the fine cotton yarn for a towel edging, take the towel with you so you can match the colors. It is very difficult to match colors from memory, and there are so many to choose from that you can either match or contrast the trim.

Materials: For a beige towel, we used Phildar Perle #5 in an off white called Chanvre, 1 ball.
Needles: #1

Directions

While most of the projects in this book are made on large needles, the edgings are worked on very small needles. In this case the projects are small and therefore still fall into the category of quick and easy.

Begin by casting on 13 sts.

Row 1 and all other odd-numbered rows: K 2, p to last 2 sts, k 2. (Number of p sts will vary on different rows.)

Row 2: Slip 1, k 3, yo, k 5, yo, k 2 tog, yo, k 2 (15 sts).

Row 4: Sl 1, k 4, sl 1, k 2 tog, psso, k 2, (yo, k 2 tog) twice, k 1 (13 sts).

Row 6: Sl 1, k 3, sl 1, k 1, psso, k 2, (yo, k 2 tog) twice, k 1 (12 sts).

Row 8: Sl 1, k 2, sl 1, k 1, psso, k 2, (yo, k 2 tog) twice, k 1 (11 sts).

Row 10: Sl 1, k 1, sl 1, k 1, psso, k2, (yo, k 2 tog) twice, k 1 (10 sts).

Row 12: K 1, sl 1, k 1, psso, k 2, yo, k 1, yo, k 2 tog, yo, k 2 (11 sts).

Row 14: Sl 1, (k 3, yo) twice, k 2 tog, yo, k 2 (13 sts).

Repeat rows 1 to 14 until you reach desired length. Bind off.

Finish: Position edging on the lower hem of towel and backstitch around all edges.

Guest towel with scalloped edging

This towel matches the previous towel in color, but the edging is narrower and scalloped for variety. It's nice to have them match in color but create each individually with different trims.

Materials: For a beige towel, use Phildar Perle #5 in an off white called Chanvre or ecru, 1 ball (or leftover yarn from project on page 106).
Needles: #1

Directions

Cast on 6 sts.

Row 1: K 3, yo, sl 1, k 2 tog, psso (5 sts).

Row 2: K in front, back and front of first st; p 3, k 1 (7 sts).

Row 3: K 2, (yo, sl 1, k l, psso) twice; k 1.

Row 4: K in front and back of first st, p 5, k 1 (8 sts).

Row 5: K 1 (yo, sl 1, k 1, psso) 3 times; k 1.

Row 6: K 2 tog, p 5, k 1 (7 sts).

Row 7: Repeat row 3.

Row 8: K 2 tog, p 4, k 1 (6 sts).

Repeat these 8 rows for pattern until desired length is reached. Bind off loosely.

Finish: Position edging on lower hemline of towel and back stitch along side and top edges.

top: seashore   below: scallop edge

Decorative towel edging

This openwork knitted edging can be used for decorating a variety of items. Here it finishes off the end of a hand towel, but you might consider this pattern for a blanket trim or pillow as well.

Materials: Coats & Clark Luster Sheen—red.
Needles: #5

Directions

Starting at narrow edge, cast on 11 sts. Purl row, then work in pattern as follows:
Row 1: K 3, k 2 tog, yo twice, k 1, yo twice, sl st, k 1, psso, k 3 (13 sts).

Row 2: K 1, p 3, p 1st yo and drop 2nd yo, p 1, p 1st yo and drop 2nd yo, p 3, k 1 (11 sts).
Row 3: K 2, k 2 tog, yo twice, k 3, yo twice, sl st, k 1, psso, k 2.
Row 4: K 1, p 9 dropping 2nd yo, k 1.
Row 5: K 1, k 2 tog, yo twice, k 5, yo twice, sl st, k 1, psso, k 1.
Row 6: Repeat row 4.
Repeat rows 1 through 6 of pattern. Work in pattern for desired length. Bind off loosely.

Finish: Pin edging to towel and stitch all edges. Tack here and there to hold in position.

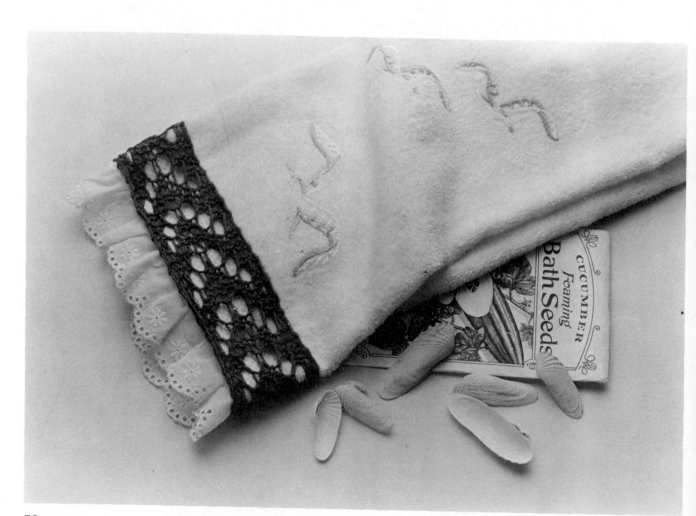

Knit everyone's favorite toy for your favorite child. The red pants are knit right into the teddy bear's body, but his white turtleneck sweater is removable.

Materials: Phildar Leader acrylic yarn—1 skein buffalo, 1 skein red, 1 skein white (for sweater); polyfil stuffing; 2 button eyes; black yarn for mouth and nose.

Needles: #8

Gauge: 5 sts = 1 inch
6 rows = 1 inch

Directions

Legs

Make 2. Cast on 18 sts of brown (buffalo color) and knit 8 rows in stockinette st (k 1 row, p 1 row).

Change to red. Inc 1 st each edge, repeat every 4th row 2 times. Continue in stockinette st until entire leg is 3 inches long.

Break off yarn. Put sts on stitch holder.

Fold each leg in half with seams on outside. Pick up front 12 sts from outside edge to inside crotch, placing remaining 12 sts on safety pin.

Cast on 3 sts. Pick up 12 sts from crotch to outside edge of front of other leg. Put remaining 12 sts on safety pin.

Continue knitting front 27 sts in red stockinette st for 3 more inches. Change to brown yarn and continue in st st for 3 inches to finish torso. Bind off loosely.

Repeat on back of legs, picking up 12 sts from one safety pin, 3 cast-on sts and 12 from the other safety pin, to make a total of 27 sts for back of pants and upper torso.

Arms

Make 2 in brown (buffalo).

Cast on 16 sts.

Work stockinette st for 3 inches.

Cut yarn, leaving 8-inch tail, and thread through loops of last row of sts.

Pull, gathering tightly, and stitch up side seam.

Head

Make 2 in brown (buffalo).

Cast on 14 sts.

Row 1: Purl.

Row 2: Inc in first st with yarn in back, k to last 2 sts, inc in next st, k 1.

Row 3: Inc in first st with yarn in front, p to last 2 sts, inc in next st, p 1.

Repeat rows 2 and 3 two more times (26 sts).

Work 14 rows in stockinette st, ending with a p row.

Decreasing rows: Dec once at each end of the next 6 rows.

Next row: Purl. Bind off and leave 10 inches for sewing.

Ears

Make 2 in brown.

Cast on 12 sts.

Row 1: Purl across.

Row 2: K 1, inc 1 in next st, k 3, inc 1 in each of next 2 sts, k 3, inc 1 in next st, k 1 (16 sts).

Row 3: Purl across.

Row 4: K 1, inc 1 in next st, k 5, inc 1 in each of next 2 sts, k 5, inc 1 in next st, k 1 (20 sts).

Row 5: Purl across.

Row 6: Knit across.

Repeat rows 5 and 6 once. Repeat row 5 again.

Row 10: K 1, k 2 tog, k 5, k 2 tog twice, k 5, k 2 tog, k 1 (16 sts).

Row 11: Purl across.

Row 12: K 1, k 2 tog, k 3, k 2 tog twice, k 3, k 2 tog, k 1 (12 sts).

Row 13: Purl across.

Row 14: K 2 tog across row and at same time bind off, leaving 10-inch tail.

Nose

Cast on 20 sts in brown.

Row 1: Purl across.

Row 2: K 2 tog across row.

Row 3: Purl across.

Row 4: K 2 tog across. Cut yarn, leaving tail, and pull through 5 remaining loops. Gather and sew closed.

Finish: With right sides of body and legs together, stitch along edges, leaving top of body open. Stitch crotch closed. Turn right side out. Repeat with each piece for arms, ears, and head, leaving the cast-on edge open for stuffing and attaching to body.

Stuff body and legs so they are quite full. Stuff arms, ears, and head and attach to the body.

Sew eyes into place. Embroider round black circle on the end of nose, and use a running stitch for outline down center and around each side of nose. See drawing of face placement.

Teddy sweater

Needles: #6 and #8
Gauge: 5 sts = 1 inch
       6 rows = 1 inch

Directions

Back
  Cast on 30 sts to #6 needles. Work 6 rows k 1, p 1.
  Change to #8 needles and work in stockinette st (k 1 row, p 1 row) until entire piece is 3 inches, ending with a p row.
Next row: K 1, sl 1, k 1, psso, knit across to last 3 sts, k 2 tog, k 1 (decrease row).
Next row: Purl.
  Repeat last 2 rows 5 times (18 sts). Put remaining sts on holder.

Front
  Same as back.

Sleeves
  Make 2.

  Cast on 22 sts. With #6 needles work 6 rows k 1, p 1.
  Change to #8 needles and work in stockinette st until entire piece is 2¼ inches, ending with a p row.
Next row: K 1, sl 1, k 1, psso, knit across to last 3 sts, k 2 tog, k 1.
Next row: Purl.
  Repeat last 2 rows 5 times (10 sts remaining).
  Put remaining sts on holder.
  Sew raglan seams connecting sleeves to front and back, leaving any one seam open. With piece open put all sts from holders onto #6 needles. Work 2 inches of k 1, p 1. Bind off loosely.
  Sew remaining seam, sleeve and side seams.
  Add a decorative appliqué or a little pocket of felt if desired.

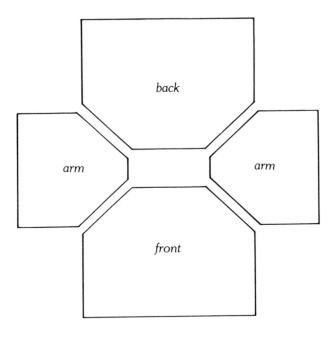

A classic his or her sweater

This classic turtleneck sweater can be made for a man or woman, and can be altered to be as simple or detailed as you wish. Use the basic pattern and vary the neckline, or run a cable stitch down the outer length of each sleeve as we did on the variation of this pattern. (See page 58.)

Materials: Tahki Kerry Donegal tweed knitting worsted—6 skeins (7 for medium) (8 for large).
Needles: #6 and #8, dp needles #6
Gauge: 9 sts and 12 rows = 2 inches on #8 needles

Directions

Back

With #6 needles, cast on 84 (92) (100) sts. Work in k 1, p 1 ribbing for 3 inches. Change to #8 needles and work in stockinette (k 1 row, p 1 row) until you have a piece that measures 15½ (16) (16½) inches from bottom edge to underarm. End on wrong side.

Shape raglan armhole: Bind off 2 sts (3) (4) at beg of next 2 rows.
Next row: K 2, sl 1, k 1, psso. K across to last 4 sts, k 2 tog, k 2 (dec row). Purl a row back.
Next Row: Purl.
Repeat last 2 rows 26 (28) (30) more times—26 (28) (30) leftover sts. Place remaining sts on holder for back neck.

Front

Work same as back until 20 (22) (24) armhole dec rows have been worked, ending right side—40 (42) (44) sts.
Shape Neck: P 10 (11) (12), place next 20 sts on holder. Join another ball of yarn, work across.

Working each side separately, dec 1 st at each neck edge every other row 3 (4) (5) times; *at the same time* continue to dec at each armhole edge as before until all sts are dec.

Sleeves

Make 2. With #6 needles, cast on 40 (42) (44) sts. Work in k 1, p 1 ribbing for 3 inches.
Next row: P across, inc 2 (4) (6) sts evenly spaced—42 (46) (50) sts.
Change to #8 needles and work in stockinette, increasing 1 st each edge every 1 (¾) (1) inch 11 (14) (13) times—64 (74) (76) sts. Work even until 18 (18½)

(19) inches from beg or desired length to underarm, ending wrong side.

Shape cap of raglan: Work as back armhole shaping until 8 sts remain. Place sts on holder.

Finishing: Set sleeves into armholes at front and back. Sew side seams and sleeves.

Neck Band: With right side facing, use dp needles to pick up and k 80 (84) (88) sts around neck edge including sts from holders.

Work in k 1, p 1 for 6 inches. Bind off loosely in ribbing.

Cable sleeve sweater

This is a variation of the classic sweater on page 56. All directions are identical for front and back pieces.

Sleeves

Make 2. Use #6 needles to cast on 40 (42) (44) sts. Work in k 1, p 1 ribbing for 3 inches.

Increase 2 (4) (6) evenly across last row of ribbing— 42 (46) (50) sts. Change to #8 needles.

Row 1: K 17 (19) (21), place a marker, p 2, k 6, p 2, place a marker, k 17 (19) (21).

Row 2: P 17 (19) (21), slip marker, k 2, p 6, k 2, p 17 (19) (21).

Repeat rows 1 and 2 throughout, working cable (see page 21) every 6th row and increasing each edge every 1 (¾) (1) inch 11 (14) (13) times—64 (74) (76) sts. Work until desired length to underarm, ending wrong side. Shape raglan cap as on page 66.

Finish: Assemble as page 56.

Neck: With right side facing, use dp needles to pick up and k 80 (84) (88) sts around neck edge, including sts from holders.

Work in k 1, p 1 for 2 inches. Bind off loosely in ribbing. Fold neck band in half lengthwise and sl st to inside.

Warm winter socks for baby

The little "work" socks are made to fit a 1- to 2-year-old. They are soft and warm and can be made with any 2 colors. Once you've made a pair, you'll want to make several to match all of baby's outfits. Unlike most sock patterns, which use 4 needles, this pattern is worked out for 2 needles and will go fast on the large size indicated.

Materials: Small amounts of Phildar Pegase red and gray yarn.
Needles: #9
Gauge: 7 sts = 2 inches
       5 rows = 1 inch

Directions

Make 2. With gray yarn cast on 25 sts.
Knit 4 inches of ribbing (k 1, p 1).
Attach red yarn. With first 8 sts only, knit 1 inch stockinette stitch (k 1 row, p 1 row).

Turn heel: Starting with outside edge.
K 1 st, k 2 tog, k 1, turn, return purling.
K 2 sts, k 2 tog, k 1, turn, return purling.
K 3 sts, k 2 tog, k 1, turn, return purling.
K 3, k 2 tog (4 sts) and pick up 4 sts on inside edge of heel. Leave the 8 sts on holder, along with next 9 sts.
Follow same procedure for 8 sts on left side, as follows:
Attach red yarn and work in stockinette stitch for 1 inch. Starting at outside edge:
P 1, p 2 tog, p 1, turn, return knitting.
P 2, k 2 tog, p 1, turn, return knitting.
P 3, k 2 tog, p 1, turn, return knitting.
P 3, p 2 tog (4 sts), and pick up 4 sts on inside edge of heel. Pick up all other sts from holder (25 sts).
Attach gray yarn. Work 2 rows stockinette st.
Next row: K 7, k 2 tog, k 7, k 2 tog, k 7 (23 sts).
Next row: Purl.
Next row: K 6, k 2 tog, k 7, k 2 tog, k 6 (21 sts).
Next row: Purl.
Continue in stockinette st for 2 inches.

Toe
Join red yarn. Work 2 rows stockinette st.
Next row: K 1, k 2 tog, k 7, k 2 tog, k 6, k 2 tog, k 1 (18 sts).
Next row: Purl.
Next row: K 1, k 2 tog, k 6, k 2 tog, k 5, k 2 tog, k 1 (16 sts).
Next row: Purl.
Next row: K 1, k 2 tog, k 2, k 2 tog, k 1, k 2 tog, k 2, k 2 tog, k 1 (11 sts).
Pull yarn through remaining 11 sts. Sew seam.

Baby's jacket sweater

This is a wonderfully warm and at the same time soft outdoor sweater for a baby size 6 to 18 months. You can choose your color combination, but for a change of pace we used off white as the background, with the trim in aqua and gray-brown. The matching socks are warm enough for outdoor wear (to replace traditional booties) and resemble woolen work socks for big people.

The edging and buttonholes are made with crochet stitches that are easily added (see pages 106–109 for details).

Materials: Phildar Pegase 206—1 skein color A: aqua (#25 Cosmos); 3 skeins color B: ecru (off white); 1 skein color C: gray (#15 Bison); 5 buttons.
Needles: #9; crochet hook #I
Gauge: 7 sts = 2 inches
         5 rows = 1 inch

Directions

Work in one piece starting from the neck. With blue (color A) cast on 50 sts. Work 2 rows garter stitch (all k). Change to white (color B). Working on wrong side, p 10 sts, place marker on needle, p 6, place marker on needle, p 18, place marker on needle, p 6, place marker on needle, p 10.
Right side: K across, inc 1 st on each side of each marker (8 inc).
Wrong side: P across.
Repeat these 2 rows until there are 114 sts on needle (18-22-34-22-18), ending on wrong side.
Next, k 2 rows in gray (color C) for stripe.
Divide for sleeves: K across first 18 sts, put on holder, continue across next 22 sts. Leave rest on a second holder.
Knit these 22 sts in stockinette (k 1 row, p 1 row) for sleeve until 5 inches long.
Attach blue (A) yarn. Knit 4 rows. Bind off.
Put sts from second holder onto needle.
Work across 34 sts for back. Put on holder.
Continue across 22 sts for other sleeve. Put remaining 18 sts on holder.
Work 2nd sleeve in same manner as first.

Body
Put all sts from holders (18-34-18) on needle—70 sts. Work in stockinette stitch:

8 rows white (B)
2 rows blue (A)
3 rows (B)
K 2 rows blue (A) garter stitch
3 rows st st white (B)
7 rows gray (C)
5 rows (B)
With blue (A) work 4 rows in garter st (all k). Bind off.

Finish: Sew sleeve seams. (See page 23.) With blue: Single crochet along left edge of front. (See page 70 for crocheting directions.)

Buttonholes: Right edge, with blue, starting at neck: sc, ch 5, 1 sl st in first of ch 5 (first buttonhole). Continue sc down edge, repeating button loop every 2 inches or where desired (5 loops shown here). Attach buttons to left edge opposite buttonholes.

Matching socks

This pattern is a slight variation from the first pair of socks found on page 60. Follow the directions up to heel, using ecru color. Use gray for heel. Continue with 8 rows in ecru.

Toe variation
Join blue yarn and work 1 row blue and 1 row ecru in stockinette stitch.
Join gray yarn (C) and complete toe as per page 60.

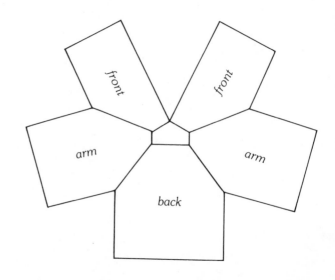

Chelsea sweater set

A sweater and matching cap can be a perfect complement for any suit. This set, designed by Robin Murray, is especially soft and lovely because of the silk-and-wool-blend yarn.

Directions are given for a small size (6–8). Changes for sizes medium (10–12) and large (14–16) are in parentheses.

Materials: (for sweater) Tahki's Chelsea silk and wool—3 (3) (4) skeins pink #117, 1 skein white #111.
Needles: #6 and #8
Gauge: With #8 needles 4 sts = 1 inch
6 rows = 1 inch
Finished bust measurement: 34 inches (36½) (39½)
Stitch Pattern:
Multiples of 3, plus 2 (use pattern at end of each row).
Color sequence:
Rows 1 and 2 main color (pink)
Rows 3 and 4 contrasting color (white)
Row 1: P across (pink).
Row 2: K 4, pass 2nd st over 3rd and 4th, * yo, k 3, pass first st over 2nd and 3rd, rep from * across row.
Row 3: P across (white).
Row 4: K 2, * yo, k 3, pass first stitch over 2nd and 3rd, repeat from * across row.

Directions

Back

With #6 needles cast on 59 (65) (71) sts in pink. Work k 1, p 1 ribbing for 2 inches, ending with wrong side. Change to #8 needles and work in stockinette stitch (k 1 row, p 1 row) until the piece measures 13 inches from the beginning, or desired length to underarm; end ready for a right-side row.

Shape armholes: Bind off 3 sts at beg of each of next 2 rows—53 (59) (65) sts. Then dec 1 st each end every other row by k 2 tog, 3 times on purl row—47 (53) (59) sts.

Yoke: Starting with row 2 of stitch pattern, work yoke with the 4 rows of the pattern, changing color every 2 rows (according to color sequence) until armholes measure 7 (7½) (8) inches ending ready for purl row. Change to #6 needles. Work 4 rows of ribbing. Bind off loosely.

Front

Work the same as back until 5 inches above armhole, ending with a p row. Working the first 15 (17) (19) sts only, k across to another needle. Keep the color sequence.

Neck edge: Dec 1 st at neck edge twice, then dec 1 st at neck edge every other row 5 times, leaving 8 (10) (12) sts to be put on holder.

Attach yarn with all the other sts and k across 17 (19) (21) sts in pattern for neck opening, put on holder. K next 2 sts tog and continue in pattern across the row. Dec again at the neck edge next row, then dec 1 st at neck edge every other row 5 times, leaving 8 (10) (12) sts to be put on holder.

With #6 needles pick up shoulder stitches from holder, pick up 8 sts around neck, pick up 17 (19) (21) sts from center holder, 8 sts around other neck edge, and sts from remaining holder. Work 4 rows of ribbing and bind off loosely.

Sleeves

Make 2. With main color (pink), cast 36 (40) (44) sts onto #6 needles. Work ribbing (k 1, p 1) for 1 inch, inc 8 sts evenly across the last row. Change to #8 needles. Starting with row 1 and main color (pink), work stitch pattern through row 4 and then do rows 1 and 2 once more (6 pattern rows).

Continue in stockinette stitch until the entire length is 3 inches. Bind off 3 sts at beg of each of next 2 rows.

Continue in stockinette until the entire length is 6½ (7) (7½) inches, ending with k row. P 2 sts tog across the next row. Next row, k 2 sts tog and at the same time bind off loosely.

Finish: Block (see page 23), press lightly.

Sew shoulders together for approximately 3 inches from armhole, overlapping ribbing from front to back. Open sweater so it lies flat and sew in sleeves. With right sides together sew side and sleeve seams. (See page 23.)

Cap

Materials: Tahki's Chelsea silk and wool—1 skein pink, small amount of white (left over from sweater).
Needles: #6 and #8

Directions

Using main color (pink), cast 90 sts onto #6 needles. Work in ribbing (k 1, p 1) for 4 rows, inc 8 sts evenly across the last row. Starting on wrong side and continuing with main color, work the 4 rows of the stitch pattern (from sweater, page 64) and then rows 1 and 2 again (6 rows of pattern). Continue in stockinette st until piece measures 5 inches.

Decreasing: Starting with right side, every 10th st k 2 tog while knitting across (90 sts). P across next row.

Every 9th st k 2 tog while knitting across (81 sts). P across next row.

Every 8th st k 2 tog while knitting across (72 sts). P across next row.

Every 7th st k 2 tog while knitting across (63 sts). P across next row.

Every 6th st k 2 tog while knitting across (54 sts). P across next row.

Every 5th st k 2 tog while knitting across (45 sts). P across next row.

Every 4th st k 2 tog while knitting across (36 sts). P across next row.

Every 3rd st k 2 tog while knitting across (27 sts). P across next row.

Every 2nd st k 2 tog while knitting across (18 sts).

Cut yarn, leaving 4 inches, and pull through remaining sts. Sew seam.

Infant sweater with hearts

It's especially fun to make a little garment for a baby or small child. And there is nothing nicer than a handmade gift for the new baby. This sweater is designed for a newborn (with the sleeves turned up) and will fit up to 6 months. Directions are given in parentheses to increase the size for 6 months to a year.

The color combination is unusual in peach and raspberry, and the heart theme on the bands can be knit right in or embroidered afterward.

The open front edges and button loops are trimmed with a single crochet stitch, and if you turn to page 70 you'll find easy directions for doing this.

Materials: Phildar Pegase #206—3 skeins #31 Champagne (peach), 1 skein #53 Lupin (raspberry); 3 buttons.
Needles: #5

Gauge: 10 sts = 2 inches
15 rows = 2 inches

Directions

The abbreviation M 1 is used here to mean make 1 stitch. It is a way of saying increase by 1—k 2 sts in 1 st. The abbreviations RS and WS mean right side and wrong side, respectively.

Working in one piece and starting at the neck with raspberry (contrasting color, B), cast on 50 (52) sts.

Work 3 rows garter stitch (all knit). Change to main color (A).

Raglans

Row 4: K 11 (12), M 1, <u>k 2</u>, M 1, k 2, M 1, <u>k 2</u>, M 1, k 16, M 1, <u>k 2</u>, M 1, k 2, M 1. <u>K 2</u>, M 1, k 11 (12)—58 (60) sts.

Mark the 4 groups of underlined k 2 with contrasting thread on the needle.

Work 3 rows. Inc 8 sts (1 st on each side of each marked group) on next and every 4th row, until there are 90 (100) sts. Work 1 row.

Continue inc in the same way on next and every other row until there are 170 (180) sts.

Sleeves

Next row: (right side of work) K 61 (65); leaving remaining 109 (115) sts on holder, turn.
Next row: K 1, M 1, k 32 (34), M 1, k 1; leaving remaining 27 (29) sts on holder for right front; turn.
** Continue on these 36 (38) sts for right sleeve and work for 5½ (6) inches, ending with contrasting color (B) for 4 rows all knit. Bind off.

With right side facing, rejoin main color to 109 (115) sts on first holder.

K 82 (86); leaving remaining 27 (29) sts on holder for left back, turn.
Next row: K 1, M 1, k 32 (34), M 1, k 1; turn, leaving remaining 48 (50) sts on holder for back.

Work left sleeve as right sleeve from ** to "Bind off."

With right side up, rejoin main color (A) and k the 27 (29) sts of left back and knit to end.

Body

With wrong side p 27 (29) from left front. P 48 (50) from back, k 27 (29) from right front—102 (108) sts.

Heart band pattern
•(Right side) K 1 row with contrasting color (B).
(Wrong side) K 1 row with B.
(Right side) K 1 row with main color (A).
(Wrong side) P 1 row with A.

Start heart pattern:
Row 1: (RS) 2 sts A, * 3 sts B, 1 st A, 3 B, 3 A. Repeat from * across, ending with 1 (3) A.
Row 2: (WS) 3 A (1 A), 7 B, * 3 A, 7 B. Repeat from * across, ending 2 A.
Row 3: (RS) 3 A, 5 B, * 5 A, 5 B. Repeat from * across, ending with 4 A (2 A).
Row 4: (WS) 5 A (3 A), 3 B, * 7 A, 3 B. Repeat from * across, ending with 4 A.
Row 5: (RS) 5 A, 1 B, * 9 A, 1 B. Repeat from * across, ending with 6 A (4 A).

Row 6: (WS) P in main color (A).
Row 7: (RS) K in main color (A).
Row 8: (WS) K in contrasting color (B).
•**Row 9:** (RS) K 1 row (garter st) (B).
Do 9 rows in stockinette st in A, starting with a p row.
Next row: (RS) K in B.
Next row: (WS) K in B.
Repeat entire pattern between black dots, reversing colors. End with 2 more rows of k in main color (A). Bind off.

Finish: Join sleeve seams.

With right side facing and using contrasting color (B), work a row of sc on one front edge. (See pages 69–75 for crocheting directions.) Fasten off. On opposite front edge attach yarn, ch 5 for buttonhole lp, sl st into first of ch 5. Continue along edge in sc; every 2½ inches make another ch 5 for buttonhole loop. Fasten off.

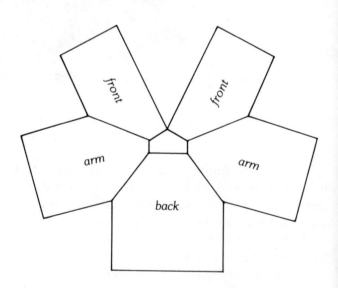

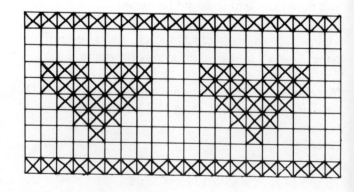

Getting started in crochet

Most of the projects made in crochet can be achieved with a few basic stitches. All the work starts with a chain made up of a series of loops on a crochet hook. Unlike knitting, which is done on two, three and sometimes four needles, crocheting is done on a single hook. Hooks come in various sizes. The size you use will depend on the yarn, pattern and item.

Most yarn used for knitting can also be used for crocheting. However, the very fine crochet cotton is best for the fine lacy items made with crochet stitches rather than knitting.

Chain stitch

All projects here begin with the chain stitch.

1. Make a slip knot by taking yarn about 2 inches from end and winding it once around your middle three fingers.

2. Pull a length of yarn through the loop around your fingers. Put this new loop on your crochet hook and pull tight.

3. With yarn wound over left-hand fingers, pass the hook under the yarn on your index finger and catch a strand with the hook.

4. Draw the yarn through the loop already on the hook to make one chain stitch. Repeat steps 3 and 4 for as many chain stitches as needed. If you hold the chain as close to the hook as possible with the thumb and index finger of your left hand, the chain will be even.

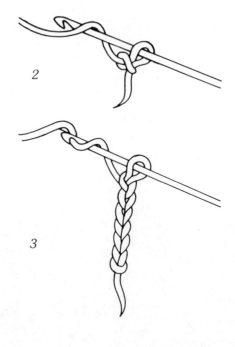

Single crochet

The beginning of every project in crochet is a row of a specific number of chain stitches. These are the basis of the piece, just as the cast-on row is the basis of a knit piece.

At the beginning of every row an extra chain stitch is made. This is counted as the first stitch of the row, and is called the turning chain.

1. After making the initial chain, insert hook in second chain from the hook (the skipped chain is the turning chain) and bring the yarn over the hook from back to front (clockwise). Pull the yarn over through the chain so you have two loops on the hook. (Note that in these instructions, each chain stitch is simply called a chain. Where a string of chain stitches is being discussed, it is known by the numbers of stitches—for example, "first ch 5" means the first group of 5 chain stitches in a row.)

2. Wind the yarn around the hook again and draw the hook with its 3rd loop through the two loops already on the hook. You have made one single crochet (sc).

3. Continue to work a single crochet in each chain stitch. At the end of the row, make one chain (ch 1) and turn your work around from right to left so the reverse is facing you.

4. The turning chain stitch counts as the first stitch. Work the next single crochet by inserting your hook through the top loop of the next stitch in the previous row. Wind the yarn over the hook (yo) and draw it through the stitch. Yarn over and through two loops on hook. Continue to work a single crochet in each stitch across row. Chain 1 and turn.

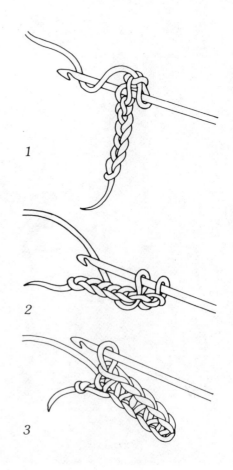

Fastening off

At the end of all required rows or rounds, cut the yarn with a tail of 2 or 3 inches and draw it through the last loop at the end of the row. Pull tightly and weave it into the fabric with a yarn needle. Sometimes the tail is used to sew pieces together. Cut off yarn according to how the piece will be used. Sometimes you may need more to sew with.

Double crochet

1. With your foundation chain made, bring yarn over hook and insert hook in 4th chain from hook.
2. Yarn over hook. Draw through chain. There are 3 loops on hook.
3. Yarn over hook. Draw through 2 loops on hook. There are now 2 loops on hook.
4. Yarn over hook. Draw yarn through the last 2 loops on hook. One double crochet is completed. Insert hook into next stitch in foundation chain, and repeat steps 2, 3 and 4.

Once you've worked a double crochet in every chain across the row, ch 3 and turn. This turning chain of 3 chain stitches counts as one double crochet beginning the next row.
5. Skip first stitch and work double crochet (dc) in top loop of each double crochet across.
6. Work double crochet in first stitches of ch 3 (turning chain).

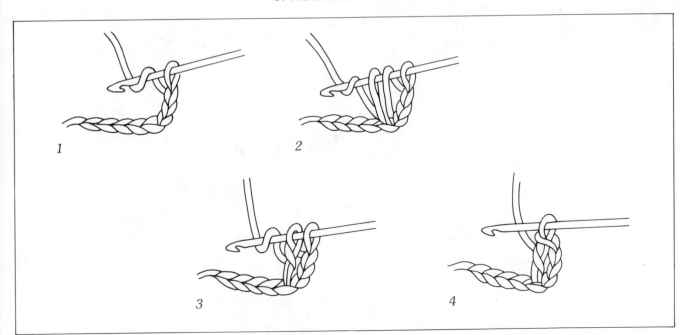

1

2

3

4

Half double crochet

Make a foundation chain.

1. Yarn over hook and insert hook through loop of third chain from hook.

2. Yarn over hook. Draw yarn through the chain so there are 3 loops on hook.

3. Yarn over hook. Draw through all 3 loops to complete half double crochet (hdc).

Continue to do this in each chain across row. At end of row, ch 2 to turn. Skip first stitch and work first half double crochet into each half double crochet across. Last hdc in row is worked in turning ch. Ch 2 to turn.

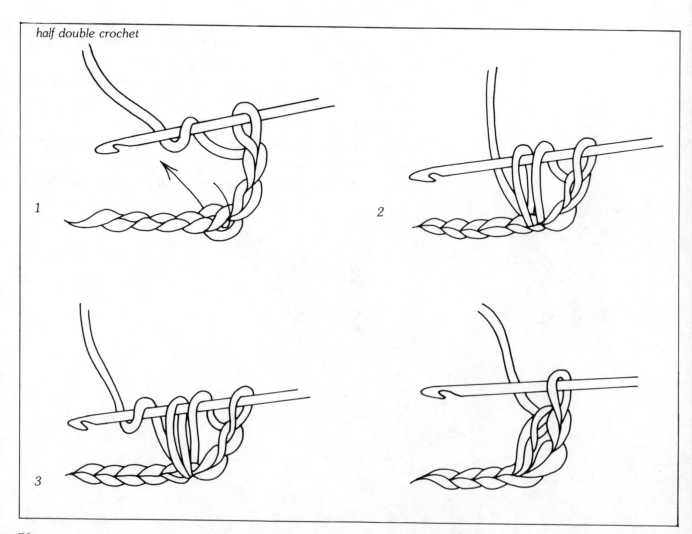

half double crochet

1

2

3

Treble or triple crochet

Make a foundation chain.

With 1 loop on your hook, put the yarn over the hook twice. Insert hook in 5th chain from the hook, yarn over hook and pull loop through. Yarn over, draw through 2 loops at once 3 times.

At end of row, ch 4 and turn. This turning chain of 4 is the first triple crochet (tr) of the next row.

Turning

Depending on the crochet stitch you are working, you will need a number of chain stitches at the end of each row to bring your work into position for the next row. For a single crochet you will ch 1 to turn, for a half double crochet you will ch 2, for a double crochet you will ch 3 and for a treble or triple crochet, ch 4.

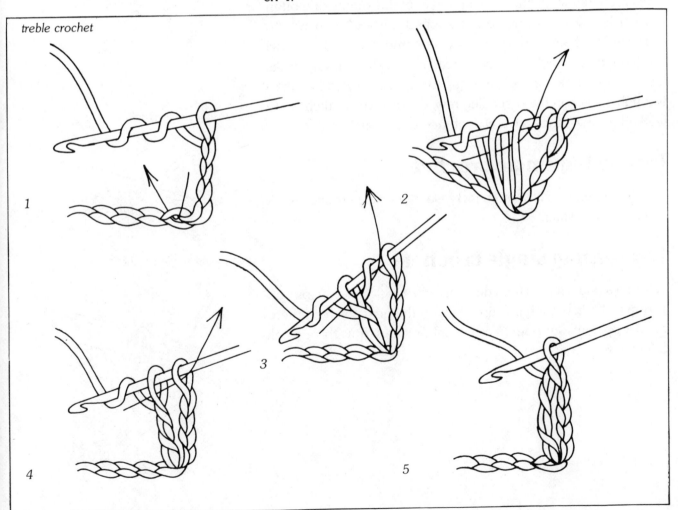

treble crochet

1

2

3

4

5

Slip stitch

Insert hook into chain. Yarn over hook and draw through both stitch and loop on hook in one motion. This completes one slip stitch (sl st). A slip stitch is used to join a chain in order to form a ring.

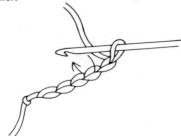

Joining rounds

If you are making a hat, for example, work to the end of the round as per directions given for the specific project. Then join by inserting hook into top loop of first stitch on same round you have been working, and work slip stitch. In this way you join the first and last stitches of the round.

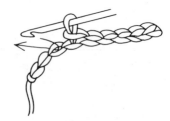

Working in spaces

In crocheted work that is lacier and contains openwork, often a stitch in the preceding row is skipped; instead, you will be instructed to chain across the gap. Sometimes your pattern asks you to work stitches in a space instead of in a stitch. In that case, insert your hook through the gap or space (sp) rather than through a stitch in the preceding row. Often several stitches are worked in one space, as a way of increasing stitches.

increasing single crochet

Increasing single crochet

When a pattern calls for an increase of a single crochet, work 2 stitches in 1 stitch.

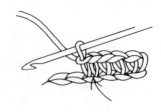

Decreasing single crochet

When a pattern calls for a decrease of a single crochet, pull up a loop in 1 stitch, then pull up a loop in the next stitch so there are 3 loops on your hook. Yarn over hook and draw through all 3 loops at once.

decreasing single crochet

Crocheting tips

Yarns

Most yarn used for knitting can also be used for crochet projects. However, the very fine crochet cotton will enable you to achieve a lacy motif that is more delicate than that which is done with traditional knitting yarns.

As with knitting, it is best to buy the amount you need to finish a project. Often the colors change slightly from one dye lot to another, and if you run out in the middle of a project you may not find the exact yarn to finish.

Gauge

Make a swatch approximately 4×4 inches using the yarn, hook and stitch pattern recommended. This will give you a chance to see the yarn made up as well as to check the gauge before beginning the project. Count the recommended stitches for the given inches and mark with pins at beginning and end. With a tape measure on the flat swatch, check to see if they correspond. If you have fewer stitches per inch than the pattern calls for, your work is too loose. Change to smaller hook. If the stitches measure more than they should, then go up one hook size. Make another swatch to be sure the gauge is correct, and adjust accordingly.

Crochet abbreviations

ch—chain
st—stitch
sts—stitches
lp—loop
inc—increase
dec—decrease
rnd—round
beg—beginning
sk—skip
tog—together
sc—single crochet
sl st—slip stitch
dc—double crochet
hdc—half double crochet
tr—treble or triple crochet
sp—space
pat—pattern
yo—yarn over hook
*—repeat what comes after
rep—repeat
() work directions in parentheses as many times as specified after parentheses. For example: (dc 1, ch 1) 3 times.

Granny square place mat

This easy-to-make place mat is crocheted with cotton yarn for easy care. The pattern can be used for many projects. Simply crochet as many squares as needed and sew together. This place mat combines 6 squares.

Materials: Phildar Abordage #322 blue color, 1 ball per place mat.
Crochet hook: #H or #8 USA

Directions

Make 6 ch and join into a ring with a sl st into first ch.

Rnd 1: Ch 3, 15 dc in sp created by ring, join with a sl st to 3rd of first ch 3.

Rnd 2: Ch 5, * 1 dc in next dc, ch 2, rep from * 14 times more. Join with a sl st to 3rd of first ch 5.

Rnd 3: Sl st in first sp, ch 3, (1 dc, ch 3, 2 dc) in same sp, * (ch 2, 1 sc in next sp) 3 times, ch 2, (2 dc, ch 3, 2 dc) in next sp, rep from * twice more, (ch 2, 1 sc in next sp) 3 times, ch 2, join with a sl st to 3rd of first ch 3.

Rnd 4: Sl st in next ch 3 sp, ch 3, (1 dc, ch 3, 2 dc) in same sp, * (ch 2, 1 sc in ch 2 sp) 4 times, ch 2, (2 dc, ch 3, 2 dc) in ch 3 sp, rep from * twice more, (ch 2, 1 sc in ch 2 sp) 4 times, ch 2, join with a sl st to 3rd of first ch 3.

Rnd 5: Sl st in ch 3 sp, ch 3, (2 dc, ch 2, 3 dc) in same sp, * (ch 1, 2 dc in ch 2 sp) 5 times, ch 1, (ch 3, ch 2, 3 dc) in ch 3 sp, rep from *twice more, (ch 1, 2 dc in ch 2 sp) 5 times, ch 1, join with a sl st to 3rd of first ch 3. Fasten off.

Stitch all squares together and finish edge of place mat with a sc all around.

Scrap yarn cap

This simple, warm cap is easy to crochet and can be made from leftover yarn; or ply a sportyarn with mohair, or do as we've done here and use one skein of Peruv' Anny from Laines Anny Blatt. The varied colors of warm brown and honey tones, with flecks of white, make the perfect combination to go with any coat or jacket.

Materials: Peruv' Anny—1 skein.
Hook: 7:00 mm or #K

Directions

Ch 4 and connect into ring with sl st into 1st ch.
Rnd 1: Ch 3, 15 dc in ring sp, join with a sl st to 3rd of beginning ch 3.
Rnd 2: Ch 3, * 2 dc in next dc, 1 dc in next dc. Repeat from * around circle, join with sl st to 3rd of beg ch 3.
Rnd 3: Ch 3 * 2 dc in next dc, 1 dc in each of next 2 dc. Repeat from * around and join with a sl st to 3rd of beg ch 3.
Rnd 4: Ch 3 * 2 dc in next dc, 1 dc in each of next 3 dc. Repeat from * around and join with sl st to 3rd of beg ch 3.
Rnd 5: Ch 3, 1 dc in each dc around, join with sl st to 3rd of beg ch 3.
Repeat round 5 until desired length.

Metallic evening purse

Crochet a little evening purse in one evening. This project is made in one piece, then folded and stitched together. It can also be lined with satin if desired.

Materials: Bucilla Spotlight—1 ball.
Hook: #G
Gauge: 6 sc = 1 inch
   6 rows = 1 inch

Note: Bag is worked vertically in one piece, and the finished project measures 5½×4½ inches.

Directions

Row 1: Ch 31, 1 sc in 2nd ch from hook and each ch across, ch 1, turn (30 sts).
Row 2: 1 sc in each sc, ch 1, turn. Rep this row 58 times (total of 60 rows), end last row. Do not fasten off. Ch 2, turn.
Purse Flap (12 rows):
Row 1: 1 hdc in 1st sc, 1 hdc in next sc, * ch 3, skip 2 sc, 1 sc in next sc, ch 3, skip 2 sc, 1 hdc in each of next 2 sc, rep from * to end, ch 2, turn.
Row 2: 1 hdc in each of first 2 hdc, * ch 3, (1 sc, ch 3, 1 sc) in next sc, ch 3, 1 hdc in each of next 2 hdc, rep from * to end, ch 1, turn.
Row 3: 1 sc in each of 1st 2 hdc, * 1 sc in ch 3 sp, ch 5, 1 sc in next ch 3 sp, 1 sc in each of next 2 hdc, rep from * to end, ch 1, turn.
Row 4: 1 sc in each of 1st 2 sc, * skip 1 sc, 7 sc in ch 5 sp, skip 1 sc, 1 sc in each of next 2 sc, rep from * to end, ch 2, turn.
Row 5: 1 hdc in each of 1st 2 sc, * ch 3, skip 3 sc, 1 sc in next sc, ch 3, skip 3 sc, 1 hdc in each of next 2 sc, rep from * to end, ch 2, turn.
 Rep rows 2 through 5 once.
 Rep rows 2 and 3 once.
Last row: 1 sc in each of 1st 2 sc, * skip 1 sc, (3 sc, ch 3, 3 sc) in ch 5 sp, skip 1 sc, 1 sc in each of next 2 sc. Rep from * to end. Fasten off.

Fold bag to beginning edge of flap and sew side seams together—or sc around the bag sides and flap edges.

Strap
 Make a 30-inch ch beginning at one top corner of the bag. Fasten at the other top corner and return with 1 sc in each chain. Fasten off.

Silver evening camisole

Crochet an evening top in the morning and wear it that night. This camisole is made to match the evening bag on page 82. You might like to make narrow straps, or weave ribbon through the top and bottom edges to wear it strapless. It can also be lined with a soft, silky fabric.

Materials: Bucilla Spotlight—3 skeins; ¼-inch elastic or ribbon.
Hook: #6

Directions

Ch 100 (small) (110 medium, 120 large), join with sl st. * Ch 2 for first dc, 1 dc in every chain. Join at 2nd of ch 2. Repeat from * until tube equals 12 (13) (14) inches or desired length from top to waist.

Since the metallic yarns have no elasticity, run ¼-inch elastic through top and waist edge, or use a matching ¼-inch ribbon as we did here.

For a variation, you can make this pattern from ¼-inch rayon ribbons by Gemini (see projects on pages 34 and 46), or with a cotton yarn such as Princess by Bernat, or Abordage by Phildar.

Evening combs

If you are making the evening bag on page 82 or the camisole top on page 84, you might like to make a flower or two to wear in your hair or to attach to a ribbon to wear as a necklace. The following directions are for making three different versions. Make one for your hair, one for the top of the camisole, one to go on the purse and another for your neck or wrist.

Materials: Leftover silver metallic Bucilla Spotlight yarn; hair combs; ribbons (optional for neck).
Hook: #3

Directions

Flower 1
   Ch 4 to form ring.
Rnd 1: Work 8 sc in ring sp. Join with sl st.
Rnd 2: Ch 3 (to replace 1 tr), * ch 3, 1 tr in sc. Repeat from * 7 times, ch 3. Join into 3rd ch of beg ch 3 (8 spokes).
Rnd 3: Work * (1 sc, 2 dc, 2 tc, 2 dc, 1 sc) on 1st spoke (tr), sl st in 1st sc of rnd 1. Repeat from * on next tr, 3 sc in each of first ch 3 *, rep between last 2 * 4 times (8 leaves). Join.
Rnd 4: Sc in each sp, tightly gathering lps tog. Fasten off.

Flower 2
   Ch 4. Join to make ring.
Rnd 1: (Sl st, ch 3). Repeat twice in each ch (8 loops).
Rnd 2: Sl st back to original ring. * (Ch 3, 3 tr, join all 4 with sl st) all in 1 back lp of original ring. Ch 3. Repeat from * 4 times. Join with sl st.
Rnd 3: In each sp work (2 sc, ch 3, 2 sc). Join and fasten off.

Flower 3
   Same as flower on front of slippers on page 38. Use #3 crochet hook.

Finish
   Attach flower to hair comb or run ribbon through back of flower to tie around neck.

Carriage blanket

This baby's blanket is warm and fluffy and is made with a ply of mohair and wool. You can use a mohair blend such as Phildar's Anouchka or Dedicace plied with a contrasting worsted for the same effect.

The border is created with small granny squares, and the same pattern is repeated in the large squares that make up the main part of the blanket. The decorative roses add a contrasting touch, and can be repeated in reverse colors on the matching pillow (see page 91).

Materials: 5 skeins worsted or wool in ecru color, 5 skeins ecru mohair (not necessary, but makes the blanket softer and more luxurious), 2 skeins worsted in a contrasting color (here we used aqua).

Hook: #1

Directions

Main squares

Make 2. You will be working with one strand worsted and one strand mohair.

Beg at center, ch 6. Join with sl st to form ring.

Rnd 1: Ch 3, work 2 dc in ring sp, (ch 3, 3 dc, making one shell in ring) 3 times, ch 3. Join with sl st to top of 1st ch 3. Sl st in next 2 dc, sl st in next sp.

Rnd 2: Ch 3; in same sp work 2 dc, ch 3 and 3 dc (first corner), * ch 1, in next corner sp work 3 dc, ch 3 and 3 dc (another corner). Repeat from * twice more, ch 1, join with sl st to top of ch 3. Sl st in next 2 dc, sl st in next sp.

Rnd 3: Work 1st corner in same sp, * (ch 1, shell in next ch 1 sp). Repeat from * across to next corner, work corner, repeat (ch 1, shell) to corner, repeat corner, repeat (ch 1, shell) to corner, repeat corner, repeat (ch 1, shell) to 1st corner. Join with sl st top of ch 3.

Rnds 4 through 12: Continue as in rnd 3 with main color until 12 rounds have been completed. Fasten off.

Border squares

Make 22. Using contrasting color (aqua), ch 4 and join into a ring with a sl st in first ch.

Rnd 1: *Ch 2, 4 dc in ring sp, sl st in ring, rep from * 3 times more.

Rnd 2: Sl st into back of 3rd dc; * keeping yarn at back of work, ch 4, sl st in back of 3rd dc of next group, rep from * twice more, ch 4, join with sl st to 1st sl st.

Rnd 3: In each sp work 1 sl st, 5 dc, 1 sl st.

Rnd 4: * Ch 6, 1 sl st in back of sl st between petals, rep from * 3 times more. Attach main color.

Rnd 5: Ch 3, (2 dc, ch 3, 3 dc) in same sp, * ch 1, (3 dc, ch 3, 3 dc) in next sp, rep from * twice more, ch 1, join with a sl st to 3rd of 1st ch 3.

Rnd 6: Ch 3, (2 dc, ch 3, 3 dc) in same sp, *ch 1, 3 dc in ch 1 sp, ch 1, (3 dc, ch 3, 3 dc) in ch 3, sp, rep from * twice more, ch 1, 3 dc to ch 1 sp, ch 1, join with sl st to 3rd of first ch 3.

Rnd 7: Ch 3, (2 dc, ch 3, 3 dc) in same sp * (ch 1, 3 dc in ch 1 sp) twice, ch 1, (3 dc, ch 3, 3 dc) into ch 3 sp, rep from * twice more, (ch 1, 3 dc in ch 1 sp) twice, ch 1, join with sl st to 3rd of 1st ch 3.

Fasten off.

Finish: Using main yarn, sew large squares together or attach with sc. Attach all small squares around outside edge and sc around entire blanket edges.

for pillow use 4 squares. colours— worsted (aqua and ecru)

aqua—square
ecru—flower and border

assembly pattern for carriage blanket

Baby pillow

This baby pillow is made to match the carriage blanket on page 88; however, you can make it to use as a decorative pillow in any two contrasting colors. For this pillow the contrasting color (aqua) from the blanket is used as the dominating color, with the ecru as the accent.

Materials: 1 skein worsted, 1 skein mohair (optional), 1 skein contrasting color worsted (aqua and ecru used here); 14-inch pillow form or polyfil stuffing; ½-yard cotton fabric to match yarn.
Hook: #I

Directions

Make 4. Follow directions for making border squares for carriage blanket on page 88, using ecru color for rnds 1 through 4. Change to aqua color for rnds 5 through 7. Join squares with sc, or sew together with matching yarn.
Outside edge: Using contrasting or ecru color, work 2 rows around joined square of (3 dc in sp, ch 1) around, and *on* corners work (3 dc, ch 1) in corner sp twice.
Shell edge: Attach contrasting or aqua color in ch 1 sp, * skip 1 dc and work 6 dc in next dc, sk 1 dc, work sl st in ch 1 sp, repeat from * around entire square. Fasten off.

Pillow
Cut 2 pieces of cotton fabric 15 inches square. With right sides together, stitch around 3 sides, leaving a ½-inch seam all around. Trim seams and cut off corners. Turn right side out. Press raw edges to inside. Stuff with pillow form or fill with polyfil stuffing and blind stitch open edge.
Stretch crocheted pillow cover over front of pillow so that scalloped edge extends slightly all around. Tack in place on pillow.

Striped cotton carryall

This versatile carryall is shaped like the standard duffel bag and is the perfect size for weekend travel. Because it's made with heavy cotton yarn, it is washable and can be used for all your beach gear.

Materials: Tahki's Creole 100% cotton yarn—3 skeins each of chrome yellow #714, purple #716, red #715; 22-inch-long zipper.
Hook: U.S. size #J or European #5.50
Gauge: 11 sc = 4 inches
         3 rows or rounds = 1 inch
         Each end circle 10 inches diameter

Directions

End circle 1

Starting with red, ch 4. Join with sl st to form ring.
Rnd 1: Ch 1, 8 sc in ring sp. Join with sl st to first sc.
Rnd 2: Ch 1, 2 sc in same sc as joining, 2 sc in each sc around. Join—16 sc.
Rnd 3: Ch 1, 2 sc in same sc as joining, * 1 sc in next sc, 2 sc in next sc—inc made. Rep from * around, ending with 1 sc in last sc. Join—24 sc.
Rnd 4: Ch 1, 2 sc in same sc as joining, * 1 sc in each of next 2 sc, 2 sc in next sc. Rep from * around, ending with 1 sc in each of last 2 sc. Join—32 sc.
Rnd 5: Ch 1, 1 sc in same sc as joining, work 1 sc in each sc around, but inc 8 sc evenly spaced around, being careful incs do not fall over incs of previous rnd. Join—40 sc.
Rnd 6: Ch 1, 1 sc in each sc but inc 8 sc evenly spaced around—48 sc. Change to purple as follows: Insert hook in 1st sc, drop red, pick up purple and draw a loop of purple through to complete joining sl st.
Rnd 7: Working with purple, ch 1; 1 sc in each sc, but inc 8 sc evenly spaced around. Join with sl st. Break off and fasten—56 sc.
Rnd 8: Pick up red yarn. Ch 1, 1 sc in each sc, inc 8 sc evenly spaced around. Join—64 sc.
Rnd 9: With yellow, ch 1, 1 sc in each sc, inc 8 sc evenly spaced around. Join—72 sc.
Rnd 10 through 12: With red, ch 1, 1 sc in each sc, inc 8 sc evenly around on each rnd. Join—96 sc.
Rnd 13: Ch 1, 1 sc in each sc around. Join—96 sc. Break off and fasten.

End circle 2

Make this end same as other end, substituting purple for red, yellow for purple and red for yellow.

Body

Using red yarn, ch 96, ch 1, turn and work 1 sc in each ch. Work back and forth until there are 7 inches of red. Fasten off. Join yellow yarn, working 1 sc in each of 96 sc for 2 inches. Fasten off. Work 1 row in purple. Fasten off. Join yellow and continue for 1 inch or 3 rows. Fasten off. Work 1 row of red. Fasten off. Join with yellow for 2 inches (6 rows). Fasten off. Join purple and continue working until there are 7 inches of purple. Join end to the bottom by working a row of sc, inserting hook into both end and body edge. Do the same for other end.

Strap

Using yellow yarn, make a chain 80 inches long. Work 1 sc in each ch to end and return, working sc in other side of chain. Work 1 row of sc in red on one side, and 1 row of purple on other side. Work 1 row of yellow around entire piece. Fasten off.

Finish: Finish off opening edge with sc in yellow. Attach zipper to inside of opening. Sew ends of strap together to create one loop. Place finished bag over center of loop and position strap on either side of the center stripes. Stitch strap all the way around the bag to within 4 inches of the opening on either side. You have now created a handle on each side of the bag. If you would like to carry the bag over your shoulder, you'll have to add several inches to the strap when making the original chain.

Bright crocheted hat

Made to match the carryall bag on page 92, this hat is fun to make and wear. Make your own with scraps of yarn or in the bright stripes of red, yellow and purple used here. This hat is made of Tahki's Creole cotton yarn, but you can use any yarn that is equal in weight.

Materials: Tahki's Creole—1 skein each of #714, #715, and #716.
Hook: U.S. #J or European #5.50

Directions

The pattern for the entire hat is as follows: The row stitches for every odd row are all sc, with even rows all dc. The colors are in a consistent sequence of red, yellow, purple.

Beginning with red, ch 5, joining with sl st.
Rnd 1: 8 sc in ring sp. Join.
Rnd 2: (yellow) Ch 2, 1 dc in joining st, work 2 dc in each sc.
Rnd 3: (purple) Ch 1, 1 sc in each dc around.
Rnd 4: (red) Ch 2 * 1 dc in next sc, 2 dc in next 3 sc. Repeat from * around.
Rnd 5: (yellow) Ch 1, 1 sc in each dc around.
Rnd 6: (purple) Ch 2, * 1 dc in each of next sc, 2 dc in next sc. Repeat from * around.
Rnd 7: (red) Ch 1, 1 sc in each dc around.
Rnd 8: (yellow), Ch 2, 1 dc in each sc around.

Repeat these last 3 rounds until desired length, changing color every row.

Fasten off.

Lacy pincushion

The basic pattern for the medallion on top of the pincushion is a circular motif. It can be repeated as many times as desired to make a pillow cover or doily. You can also continue to add on in order to enlarge the circle to make a table covering.

To make a doily, the pattern is identical; however, finer crochet cotton (#40) and a much smaller crochet hook (#14) are used for this project. The pincushion represents a quick and easy version of the finer project.

Materials: Phildar cotton Perle—1 ball #5 blue; small piece of satin or cotton fabric; polyfil stuffing.
Hook: #2.5

Directions

Rnd 1: Ch 6.
Rnd 2: Ch 2. Work 24 dc in ring sp. Join ring with sl st in 2nd ch.
Rnd 3: Ch 2, 1 dc in each dc. Join with sl st in 2nd ch.
Rnd 4: Ch 6, * skip 1 dc, 1 tr in next dc, ch 3. Repeat from * around, joining ch 3 with 3rd ch of 1st ch 6.
Rnd 5: * Ch 2, 1 dc in 1st space, ch 2, 1 dc in same sp, ch 2, sl st in tr. Repeat from * around, ending with sl st in first tr.
Rnd 6: * Ch 2, 1 hdc in next sp, ch 2, 1 dc in next sp, ch 2, 1 hdc in next sp, ch 2, sl st in sc. Repeat from * around. Fasten off.

Variation: Make multiples and sew together. To enlarge with additional rnds, sl st 3 times to dc. Ch 6, sl st in next dc. Continue around.
Rnd 7: Ch 4. * 1 dc, ch 1. Repeat from * in every ch st around.
Rnd 8: 1 sc in each dc and ch st around. Fasten off.
Rnd 9: Skip 2 dc. Work 10 dc in same sp, skip 2 dc, sl st 1. Repeat around entire circle. Fasten off.

Weave thread end through stitches and cut off excess on underside.

Cut 2 circles 6 inches in diameter from contrasting fabric. Stitch around edge with ¼-inch seam, leaving a 2-inch opening. Turn right side out and press. Fill with polyfil stuffing and sew opening. Tack medallion to top of pincushion.

The doily can also be made into a soft box to hold jewelry, and might be used as a set with the project on page 114.

Christmas doily

Here you will see an example of the same pattern worked with different material and on different size crochet hooks. The doily is made up of 37 motifs, each 1½ inches in diameter. It is done with fine crochet cotton (#40) on #14 steel hook. The enlarged pattern is made up of 7 motifs, each 3 inches in diameter. It is crocheted with heavier cotton on a #2.5 metric hook, or U.S. #1.

Materials: 1 ball bright-red cotton crochet yarn (Phildar's Perle #5).
Hook: Metric #2.5 or U.S. #1 steel

Directions

Ch 6, close ring with sl st.

Rnd 1: Ch 4, * tr in sp, ch 1. Repeat from * 15 times around circle (16 spokes). Join last ch 1 in 3rd ch of beg ch 4.
Rnd 2: Ch 1. Work 2 sc in each ch 1 sp, 1 sc in each tr around, join with a sl st into 1st ch (48 sc in total).
Rnd 3: Ch 3; 1 dc in next 3 sc, keeping last lp of each dc on hook. Yo and draw through 4 lps. * Ch 4, 4 dc in next 4 sc, keeping last lp of each dc on hook. Yo and draw through 5 lps. Repeat from *, end with sl st (12 points and 12 spaces created).
Rnd 4: Ch 1; in each space (3 sc, ch 3, sl st back into first ch, 3 sc), end with a sl st. Fasten off.
  Sew together 7 medallions.

Square medallion pillow

The pretty squares that make up this pillow cover start with a spoked wheel center, and the corners and sides are softly scalloped. You can make any number of crocheted squares to put together for doilies, table covers, even a coverlet for a bed. Each square is slightly more than 5 inches, and when 4 are put together they fit nicely on a 12-inch square pillow form. You can crochet the back or, as here, cover the pillow with satin in a contrasting color. The satin pillow is pink with the motif in deep purple.

Materials: Bernat Cassino cotton yarn—1 pull skein deep purple; 13×26-inch piece pink satin; 12-inch pillow form.
Hook: #3 or U.S. #D

Directions

Make 4. Starting at center, ch 6. Join with sl st to form ring.
Rnd 1: Ch 8, (work tr in ring, ch 4) 7 times; sl st in 4th ch of ch 8 (8 spokes).
Rnd 2: Ch 1, work 6 sc in each sp around (48 sc). Join with sl st into ch 1.
Rnd 3: Ch 1, 1 sc in next sc; (1 hdc in next sc, 1 dc in each of next 8 sc, 1 hdc in next sc, 1 sc in each of next 2 sc) 4 times, ending last repeat with 1 sc instead of 2 (4 petals with 12 sts each). Join with sl st into ch 1.
Rnd 4: Sl st in next 6 sts, ch 8, 1 sc in same st as last sl st, ch 5, skip next 3 sts, 1 sc in next st, ch 5, skip next 4 sts, 1 sc in next st, ch 5, skip next 2 sts, 1 dc in next st.* Ch 5, 1 sc in same st, ch 5, skip 3 sts, 1 sc in next st, ch 5, skip next 4 sts, 1 sc in next st, ch 5, skip next 2 sts, 1 dc in next st. Repeat from * twice more, ending last repeat by joining with sl st in 3rd ch of ch 8 instead of dc in next st.
Rnd 5: * Work 11 sc in next ch 5 corner lp; (ch 5, 1 sc in next sp) 3 times, ch 5. Repeat from * 3 times more. Join with sl st in first sc.
Rnd 6: Ch 4, 1 tr in each of next 10 sc. * Sc in next sp, (ch 5, sc in next sp) 3 times, 1 tr in each of next 11 sc. Repeat from * twice more. 1 sc in next sp, (ch 5, 1 sc in next sp) 3 times. Join with sl st in top of ch 4. Break off.

Finish: Join 2 squares together by sewing with a blunt-ended yarn needle and the yarn used for the squares. Don't pull yarn too tightly. Weave end under several stitches on wrong side.

Pillow

Cut 2 pieces of satin 13 inches square. With right sides together, stitch around 3 sides, leaving ½-inch seam. Trim and clip corners. Turn and press. Insert pillow form and sew opening. Attach crocheted piece by tacking at each corner first. Use fine thread to sew around edges of crochet to attach to pillow. Tack here and there in center of motifs.

Cording or ruffle around edges is optional.

Lap blanket

Make a lap or stadium blanket for outdoor sport watching. This afghan is created with one giant granny square crocheted on a large (#13) hook. It takes only one bag of variegated yarn to get the even change of color without having to change yarn. Tahki's Ambrosia is especially nice for this project, as the colors are nicely spaced with subtle changes that work well together.

Materials: Tahki Ambrosia II—1 bag color #619 (8 skeins).
Hook: #13

Directions

Chain 5, join with sl st to form a ring.

Rnd 1: Ch 3, 2 dc in ring sp, * ch 3, 3 dc in ring, repeat from * twice more, end with ch 3, sl st in 3rd st of 1st ch 3.

Rnd 2: Sl st to 1st sp, ch 3, (2 dc, ch 3, 3 dc) in same sp (corner), * ch 1, sk 3 dc, (3 dc, ch 3, 3 dc) in next sp, repeat from * twice, end with a ch 1 sl st in top of ch 3.

Rnd 3: Sl st to corner sp, ch 3, (2 dc, ch 3, 3 dc) in same sp. * Ch 1, 3 dc in next sp, ch 1, (3 dc, ch 3, 3 dc) in corner sp, repeat from *, end with a ch 1, 3 dc in next sp, ch 1, sl st in top of ch 3.

Rnd 4: Sl st to corner of sp, ch 3, (2 dc, ch 3, 3 dc) in same sp, * ch 1, 3 dc in 1st sp, ch 1, 3 dc in 2nd sp, ch 1, (3 dc, ch 3, 3 dc) in corner sp, repeat from * around, end with a ch 1, (3 dc in next sp) twice, ch 1, sl st in top of ch 3.

Rnd 5: Sl st to corner sp, ch 3, (2 dc, ch 3, 3 dc) in same sp, *(ch 1, 3 dc in next sp) 3 times, ch 1, (3 dc, ch 3, 3 dc) in corner sp, repeat from * around, end with a (ch 1, 3 dc in next sp) 3 times, ch 1, sl st in top of ch 3.

Continue working as for rnd 5, adding one more group of 3 dc (or 4 groups in total rnd), on each side of blanket every round. Fasten off when desired size. 24 rounds should be 48 inches.

Bright and sporty bag

This little striped bag measures 5½×9 inches, which is the perfect size to hold a few essentials when you don't want to carry a large purse. The bright color combination is fun to make and wear, but you can create any color combination that suits you. If you have lots of leftover yarn, this is the perfect project.

Materials: Coats & Clark Luster Sheen (100% washable)—1 skein each in the following colors: #172 lilac, #144 violet, #328 hot red, #490 navy; small round bead button.
Hook: #6 or #H

Directions

Make 2. Chain 30. Every row is started with 1 ch and sc across. Work piece back and forth in sc rows.

Color sequence

Hot red: 8 rows
Navy: 1 row
Violet: 3 rows
Navy: 3 rows
Lilac: 7 rows
Navy: 5 rows
Hot red: 8 rows
Navy: 2 rows
Violet: 4 rows
Navy: 2 rows
Hot red: 2 rows
Navy: 1 row
Lilac: 3 rows
Navy: 2 rows
Hot red: 8 rows

Using navy, sc pieces together around 3 sides; sc around opening edge.

To make flap, use navy and sc 10 rows. On next row sc halfway across (15 sc), ch 10, sl st into 1st ch, sc across rest of row.
Last row: Sc halfway across, 12 sc in ch 10 sp, sc across.

Attach button to front of purse.

Strap

Ch desired length for strap (30 inches here). Attach at corner and return sc in each ch. Attach at other side and fasten off.

Edging

Once you learn the basic crochet stitches, you can make a variety of edgings to individualize handmade as well as bought items. For example, add a lacy scalloped edge to a place mat, with another trim on the napkin. Or edge a plain handkerchief to make it special. The addition of a crocheted edge on guest towels makes them look like the expensive items found in boutiques. This is also a good way to add an unusual touch to a wedding gift of sheets and pillowcases.

Scalloped place mat

This place mat is store-bought and edged with a matching color crochet cotton such as Phildar's Perle #5 (pink).

Materials: 1 ball cotton yarn.
Hook: #2 steel

Directions

Rnd 1: Sc around the mat and sl st into first sc.
Rnd 2: * Ch 3, skip 2 sc, 1 sc. Repeat from * around mat. Sl st into first sc.
Rnd 3: 3 sl st in first ch 3 sp. * Ch 4, 1 sc in next sp. Repeat from * around mat. Join with sl st.
Rnd 4: 3 sl st in first ch 4 sp. * Ch 5, 1 sc in next sp. Repeat from * around mat. Join with sl st.
Rnd 5: Work 6 sc in each ch 5 sp. Join with sl st. Fasten off.

Matching napkin edge

Materials: 1 ball cotton crochet yarn (pink).
Hook: #2 steel

Directions

Rnd 1: Work 1 rnd of sc, evenly spaced on all 4 sides of napkin.
Rnd 2: * Ch 3, skip 2 sc, in next ch work (1 sc, ch 6) twice and 1 sc; ch 3, skip 2 sc, 1 sc in next ch. Repeat from * around napkin. Join with sl st.
Rnd 3: 1 sc in 1st sc and in 1 st ch 3 sp. * (Ch 3, 1 sc in next ch 6 sp) twice; ch 3, (sc in next ch 3 sp) twice; ch 3, (sc in next ch 3 sp) twice. Repeat from * across, ending with ch 3, 1 sc in last ch 3 sp, sc in last sc. Fasten off.

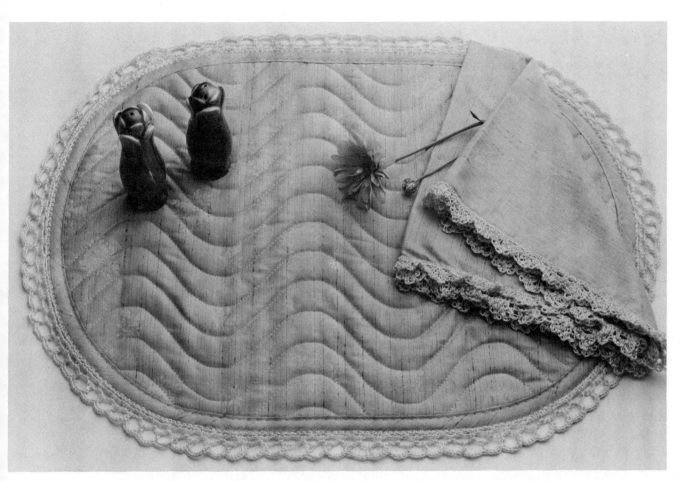

Shell-with-picot-edged place mat

The shell edging is a beautiful way to finish the edge of any fabric. It can be worked right into the material or over a base of single crochet. The picot edge can be worked as a decorative trim or to finish off an uneven edge. Here we've worked it around the finished fabric edge of a premade place mat.

Materials: Coats & Clark Luster Sheen—1 skein navy.
Hook: #2 steel

Directions

Rnd 1: Work 1 rnd of sc evenly spaced around the mat. Join with sl st.
Rnd. 2: Ch 1, 1 sc in first sc. *Ch 5, sk 3 sc, 1 sc in next sc. Repeat from * around. Join with sl st.
Rnd 3: In each ch 5 sp, work (4 dc, ch 4, 1 sc in first ch for picot, 4 dc), and in each sc work 1 sc around. Join and break off.

Picot-edged napkin

Make or buy colorful print cotton napkins to go with your crocheted place mats (see page 108). You can edge each napkin in a color to match its place mat, or choose one of the colors in the print of the napkin. The edging on this napkin is blue to match the place mat. The flowers in the print are blue, yellow and pink.

Materials: Phildar Perle #5 blue crochet cotton.
Hook: Steel #5

Directions

Rnd 1: Work 1 round of sc, evenly spaced on all 4 sides of napkin, working 3 sc in each corner.
Rnd 2: 1 sc in 1st sc. * Ch 3, sk 2 sc, in next sc work (1 dc, ch 2, 1 dc); ch 3, sk 2 sc, 1 sc in next sc. Repeat from * around (at each corner sk only 1 sc).
Rnd 3: 1 sc in 1st sc. * Ch 3, (3 sc, 4 ch, sl st in 1st ch for picot, 3 sc) in each ch 2 sp. Repeat from * around. Join with sl st in first sc.
Fasten off.

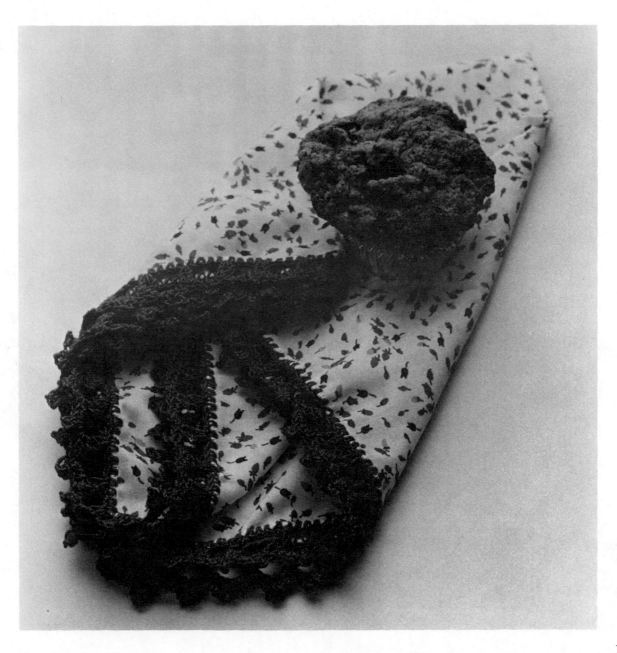

Napkin edge

Materials: Phildar Perle #5 red crochet cotton.
Hook: Steel #5

Directions

Rnd 1: Work 1 rnd of sc evenly spaced on all sides of napkin, working 3 sc in each corner. Join with sl st.
Rnd 2: Ch 3, work 1 dc at base of ch 3. * Ch 2, sk 3 sc, work 2 dc in next sc. Repeat from * around (at each corner sk only 2 sc twice). Join with sl st to top of ch 3.
Rnd 3: In each ch 2 sp work 2 sc, (ch 3, 1 sc in 1st ch for picot) and 2 sc.
    Join and break off.

Pillowcase trim

This delicate trim is perfect for sheets, pillowcases and fine towels or lingerie. It is perfect for weaving a ⅛-inch ribbon through for added interest. The scalloped shells can be placed so they extend beyond the edge of the item, or on the hemline as shown here. You can use white crochet cotton or a color to match the pillowcase.

Materials: Phildar Perle #8, white; ⅛-inch ribbon to match pillowcase.
Hook: Steel #2

Directions

Make a ch the length required, with the number of ch divisible by 3 plus 1; 2 ch, turn.
Row 1: 1 dc in 4th ch from hook, 1 dc in each ch to end.
Row 2: * Ch 3, sk next 2 dc, 1 dc in next dc. Repeat from * to end.
Row 3: Ch 3 (to equal 1 dc) and 7 dc in first sp. * 1 sc in next sp, 8 dc in next sp. Repeat from *, ending 1 sc in last sp. Fasten off.

Finish: Weave ribbon in and out of open areas. Pull out enough ribbon from center loops to make a bow. Position trim on pillowcase and stitch onto sides and top edge. Tack here and there to hold in place.

Guest towel with deep scallop edge

The trim on this guest towel is wider than the other edgings shown. It is approximately 2 inches, and is quite loose and airy with a scalloped edge. The towel is a soft peach color with matching cotton yarn.

Materials: Coats & Clark Luster Sheen crochet cotton, 1 ball to match your towel (peach used here).
Hook: Size #F or #5

Directions

Starting with narrow edge, ch 16.
Row 1: 1 dc in 8th ch from hook and in each next 8 ch. Ch 1, turn.
Row 2: 1 sc in 1st dc, (ch 5, sk next 3 dc, 1 sc in next dc) twice. Ch 7, turn.
Row 3: 1 dc in 1st sc, (ch 3, 1 sc in next sp, ch 3, 1 dc in next sc) twice. Ch 1, turn.
Row 4: 1 sc in 1st dc, (ch 3, 1 sc in next dc) twice. Ch 7, turn.
Row 5: 1 dc in 1st sc, (3 dc in next sp, 1 dc in next sc) twice. Ch 1, turn. Repeat rows 2 through 5 for desired length.

In order to finish off the raw edge, Sl st on last row, to end with ch 7 loop. Work 6 sc in each ch 7 loop across piece. Break off and fasten.

Fasten: Position edging on towel and stitch sides and top edges.

Picot-edged guest towel

Materials: Small amount of cotton crochet yarn (can be the leftover from previous project, page 112 Coats & Clark Luster Sheen, peach color).
Hook: Size #F or #5

Directions

Ch length to equal width of towel.
Row 1: Ch 2, 1 dc in each ch across piece, ch 1, turn
Row 2: 1 sc in 1st dc, * ch 5, sk 3 dc, 1 sc in each of next 3 dc. Repeat from * to end of row. 1 sc, ch 1 turn.
Row 3: Work 3 sc in each ch 5 sp, (ch 3, sc in 1st of ch) picot, work 3 sc, and make 1 sc in each of the 3 sc. End with 1 sc. Fasten off.

Finish: Position trim 1 inch from bottom edge of towel and sew together. You can tack here and there between points. Add an eyelet-and-ribbon trim above crochet if desired. Match ribbon to towel and crochet yarn.

above: picot edge below: scallop edge

Soft jewelry box

Soft boxes are made with fabric, padding and, here, a decorative crocheted medallion to top it off. The outer edge is enhanced with a 2-inch crocheted band to match. This is a beautiful way to make a variety of boxes to hold jewelry, lingerie or sewing aids, and the fabric you use can be any color or print of your choosing.

Here we used a pink satin for the outside of the box in order to show the lacy details of the crochet, which is done in olive green. The lining is a cotton print of rosy flowers with blue and beige. The crochet elements match the green leaves in the print, and when the box is opened it's a nice contrast. Since crochet yarn comes in a wide variety of shades, you'll find one to match any print used for the boxes.

Materials: Bernat Cassino—pull skein (olive green); cotton fabric and taffeta or satin (or you can line the box with the satin and eliminate the cotton)—18×18- or 9×36-inch piece of one, 18×36 of the other; quilt batting.

Hook: #5 or #F

Directions

Top

Chain 4 and join with 1 sl st to form a ring.

Rnd 1: Ch 2 (to replace 1 dc), yo, insert hook in ring sp, draw up a lp, yo, draw yarn through 2 lps, draw yarn through 3 lps on hook. This procedure is called 2 joined dc). * Ch 3, 2 joined dc. Repeat from * 7 times more, ch 3. Sl st in top of 1st 2 joined dc.

Rnd 2: In each ch 3 sp, work (1 sc, 2 dc, 1 sc). Join to beg of round to close.

Rnd 3: Sl st 3 in order to get between 2 dc. Ch 2 to replace * 1 dc between 2 dc, ch 3, 1 dc in 1st dc, ch 3. Repeat from * all around. Turn work, Sl st to join.

Rnd 4: In each ch 3 sp, work (1 sc, ch 3, 1 sc, ch 3). Sl st in 1st sc to join.

Rnd 5: * 1 sc in next ch 3 sp, ch 5, sk next ch 3 sp. Repeat from * all around, sl st in 1st sc to join.

Rnd 6: Ch 2 to replace * 1 dc in sc, 6 dc in ch 5 sp. Repeat from * all around. Sl st in 1st dc to join.

Rnd 7: 1 sc in dc, ch 7, skip 6 dc. Repeat from * all around. Sl st in 1st sc to join.

Rnd 8: In each ch 7 sp work (1 sc, 2 hdc, 2 dc, ch 1, 2 dc, 2 hdc, 1 sc). End with sl st in 1st sc to join.

Trim

Make chain 25 inches long (111) or desired length divisible by 8 plus 3. Ch 2, turn.

Row 1: 1 dc in 4th ch from hook, 1 dc in each ch to end.

Row 2: Ch 3, 1 dc in each of next 2 dc; * (ch 2, sk 2 dc, 1 dc in next dc) twice, 1 dc in each of next 2 dc, rep from * to end, working last dc in turning ch.

Row 3: Ch 4; leaving lp of each on hook, work 3 tr in next sp, yo, draw through all 4 loops on hook; * ch 9; leaving last lp of each on hook, work 3 tr in next sp, then 3 tr in next sp after the 3 dc, yo, draw through all 7 lps on hook. Rep from * to end, ending with ch 9; work a 3 dc cluster in last sp, 1 dc into turning ch.

Row 4: Sl st into top of first cluster; work (1 sc, 1 hdc, 7 dc, 1 hdc, 1 sc) in each ch 9 sp; sl st into top of last cluster.

Fasten off.

Fabric box

Top: Cut 2 9-inch circles of cotton fabric, 2 of satin and 2 of batting.

With right sides of one circle of satin and one circle of cotton fabric together, place one circle of batting on top. With a ½-inch seam allowance, stitch around edge joining all 3 layers, leaving a 2-inch opening. Trim around seam to within ¼ inch of stitching. Turn right side out with batting sandwiched between fabric. Sew opening closed.

Rim: Cut a strip of cotton fabric or satin (whichever you want on the outside of the box) 9×26 inches. Fold in half widthwise, with wrong sides together. Match short ends and stitch, leaving a ½-inch seam. This will form a ring. Cut a piece of batting 8½×25 inches. Fold in half widthwise to form ring and hand stitch short ends together.

Place batting ring inside fabric ring and fold fabric down to meet bottom edge, encasing the batting ring between the fabric. There will be an extra ½ inch of fabric at the raw edge.

Daisy pillow

Crochet a 13-petal daisy with a popcorn-stitch center and attach it to a 14-inch round pillow for a dramatic effect. The pillow is covered with a bright yellow cotton. This design can be used to create a doily as well.

Materials: Phildar Luxe—1 skein each #26 Clementine, #10 Blanc; 14-inch pillow form; 15×30-inch piece of yellow cotton fabric; 1 yard cording (optional).

Hook: U.S. #C or #2, European #3

Directions

With yellow (Clementine), ch 6, join and work 2 sc in each st of ch, join.

Rnd 2: Ch 4, 4 dc in 1 sp, sl lp off hook, insert hook in 1st dc and pull lp through. * Ch 3, 5 dc in next sc, sl lp off hook, insert in 1st dc and pull lp through (popcorn stitch). Repeat from * 10 more times, ch 3, join.

Rnd 3: Ch 1 and work 3 sc in each ch 3 loop, join and work 1 more round of sc, working into only back lp of st.

Rnd 5: Ch 3 and work a popcorn st in every other sc, with ch 3 after each popcorn st. Join.

Rnd 6: Work 5 sc in each ch 3 sp, inc 1 st in round (91 sc). Break off.

Petal

Join white (Blanc) and work 1 sc in each of the first 5 sc, ch 1, turn and work 2 rows of these 5 sc, using ch 1 each row as turning ch.

Row 4: Inc 1 st in 2nd sc; work across row and work 2 rows of sc even. Repeat rows 4–6 until there are 12 sc in row, and work 11 rows even.

Next row: Sk 1 sc, 1 sc in each remaining sc. Repeat last row until 4 sts remains. Break off.

Skip 2 sc around yellow center and work a second petal on next 5 sts. Work 11 more petals in same manner. Break off.

Finish:

Cut 2 circles of yellow fabric 15 inches in diameter. Cut a strip of fabric 2×16 inches. Cut cording same length and wrap fabric over cording with wrong sides together. With a zipper foot, stitch close to cord.

Clip seam allowance every few inches so you can ease cording around pillow. With raw edge of welting

(which is the fabric-covered cord) pinned to raw edge of right side of pillow top, machine baste together. Leave 2 inches unstitched at each end.

Open stitching at both ends of welting and overlap cording ends. Turn one end of fabric under and overlap raw end to encase cording. Baste in place.

With right sides together, pin pillow back to top (welting is between) and stitch together inside basting line. Leave a few inches open for turning and stuffing. Once it is filled with pillow form or polyfil, stitch opening closed.

Attach center of daisy to center of pillow and stitch around. Pin each petal so it lies flat on pillow and is evenly spaced from the others. Stitch around outer edge of each.

Beach bag

This nautical-looking bag is the perfect size to hold beach towel and other paraphernalia. A basic string bag, it has been designed to look like a feed bag, with the main color navy blue, then white and a few accent stripes in red. Because it is made of cotton yarn, it is light and washable.

Materials: Phildar Abordage—3 balls navy blue, 1 ball white, 1 ball red.
Hook: #8 or #H

Directions

Starting with navy, ch 6. Join with sl st to make ring.
Rnd 1: Ch 3 to equal 1 dc, 7 dc in ring (8 dc). Join with sl st at top of ch 3.
Rnd 2: Ch 3, 1 dc in first ch of ch 3, 2 dc in each dc around. Join with sl st at top of ch 3.
Rnd 3: Ch 3, 1 dc in first ch of ch 3, * 1 dc in each of next 2 dc, 2 dc in next dc. Repeat from * around. Join with sl st at top of ch 3.
Rnd 4: Ch 3, 1 dc in first ch of ch 3, * 1 dc in each of next 3 dc, 2 dc in next dc. Repeat from * around. Join with sl st at top of ch 3.

Rnd 5: Ch 3, 1 dc in first ch of ch 3, * 1 dc in each of next 4 dc, 2 dc in next dc. Repeat from * around. Join with sl st at top of ch 3.
Rnd 6: Ch 3, 1 dc in first ch of ch 3, * 1 dc in each of next 5 dc, 2 dc in next dc. Repeat from * around. Join with sl st at top of ch 3.
Rnd 7: Ch 3, 1 dc in first ch of ch 3, 1 dc in each dc all around. Join with sl st at top of ch 3.

Repeat this round for 9 inches from bottom edge. Then, working same number of sts around, follow this stripe sequence:
3 rnds dc—white
1 rnd sc—red
1 rnd dc—white
1 rnd sc—red
1 rnd dc—white
3 rnd dc—nvy
Fasten off.

Strap
Make 2. Ch 4. Turn, * ch 2, 3 dc. Repeat from * for 12 inches.

Sew to bag, with 5 inches between ends on bag. There will be approximately 9 inches between handles on either side of the bag.

Baby back pack

One large granny square is the basis for this baby's carrying pack. The yarn is cotton and will give with the child; however, it is sturdy enough to hold an infant. Make it in any color combination, or use the blue and rose colors shown here with matching straps for tying around waist and over shoulders. Once you learn the pattern, you will want to make 2 more squares for a matching diaper or carrying bag.

Materials: Tahki's cotton Creole—3 skeins each of blue (color A) and rose (color B).
Hook: #I

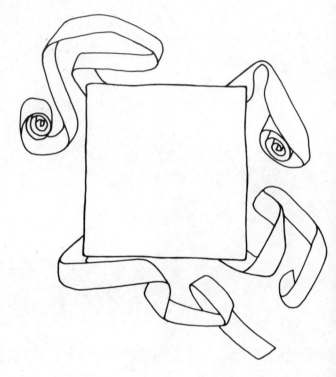

Directions

Using A, ch 8 and join into a ring with a sl st into lst ch.

Rnd 1: Using A, ch 4, 5 tr in ring sp. * Ch 3, 6 tr in ring, repeat from * twice more, ch 3, join with a sl st to 4th of ch 4.

Rnd 2: Using A, ch 5, ** yo twice, insert hook into next tr, yo, draw lp through, (yo, draw through 2 lps) twice. ** Repeat from ** to ** in each of next 4 tr, yo, draw through 6 lps. * Ch 5, 1 sl st in 2nd of ch 3, ch 5, rep from ** to ** in each of next 6 tr, yo, draw through 7 lps, rep from * twice more. Ch 5, 1 sl st in 2nd of ch 3. Break off A.

Rnd 3: Join B to top of a cluster, * work (3 tr, ch 1, 3 tr, ch 2, 3 tr, ch 1, 3 tr) in ch 3 sp of rnd 1, 1 sl st in top of next cluster, rep from * 3 times more, working last sl st in same place as yarn was joined, and joining A at the same time.

Break off B.

Rnd 4: Using A, ch 4, 5 tr in same sl st, * (6 tr, ch 2, 6 tr) in ch 2 sp, 6 tr in sl st at top of next cluster, rep from * twice more. (6 tr, ch 2, 6 tr) in ch 2 sp, join with a sl st to 4th of 1st ch 4.

Break off A.

Rnd 5: Join B to last sl st of rnd 4, ch 1, 1 sc in each of next 5 tr, 1 dc in ch 1 sp between group of tr on rnd 3, * 1 sc in each of next 6 tr, 3 sc in ch 2 sp at corner, (1 sc in each of next 6 tr, 1 dc in ch 1 sp between group of tr on rnd 3) twice. Repeat from * twice more. 1 sc in each of next 6 tr, 3 sc in ch 2 sp at corner, 1 sc in each of next 6 tr, 1 dc in ch 1 sp between group of tr on rnd 3.

Join with a sl st to lst ch.

Rnd 6: Using B, ch 3; 1 dc in each st all around, working 3 dc in center st of each corner. End by joining with sl st to 3rd of lst ch 3.

Rnd 7 and 8: Using B, repeat rnd 6.

Rnd 9 and 10: Using A, repeat rnd 6.

Rnd 11: Using A, ch 3, 1 dc in each st all along one side, working 3 dc in center st of corner.

Work 1 dc in each of next 5 sts, 1 hdc in each of next 2 sts; 1 sc in each st across side until last 8 sts; 2 hdc, 5 dc, then 3 dc in last st for corner.

Continue down 3rd side, working 1 dc in each st, 3 dc for corner.

Work (1 dc in each of next 5 sts, 1 hdc in each of next 2 sts, 1 sc in next st) across row until last 8 sts, 2 hdc, 5 dc, and 3 dc in last st for corner to complete the round.

Fasten off.

Straps

Make 2 in color A and 2 in color B. Make chain 60 inches long. 4 dc in 2nd chain from hook, 1 dc in each ch to end. 4 dc in last dc (very lst ch) and return working in other side of chain, working 1 dc in each st.

Join with sl st. Work sc around entire strap.

Fasten off.

Tote bag

This carryall bag matches the back pack on the previous pages, and is made with the same material using the same pattern. Each side reverses the color pattern. It can be used as is or lined with fabric.

Materials: Tahki Creole—3 skeins each of rose and blue; ½ yard of lining fabric; snap or 14-inch zipper for closure if desired.
Hook: #I

Directions

Make 2 squares using rnds 1 through 6 on page 122.

Rnd 7: Using B, repeat rnd 6.

Continue with 2 more rounds of dc with contrasting color.

Make one strap same as baby pack. Sc ends of strap together. With strap seam at center of bottom edge between both squares, sc edge of strap to edge of front and back squares. Carrying strap above squares will measure approximately 26 inches long.

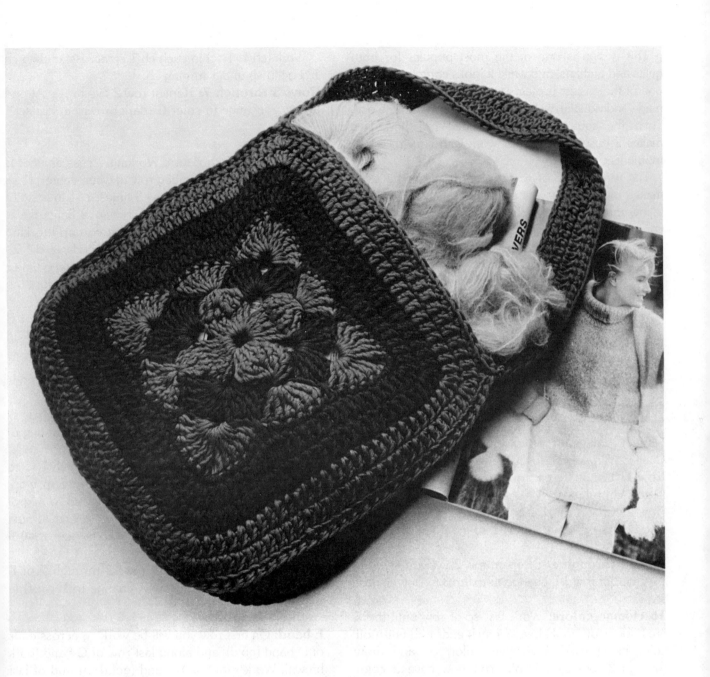

Log cabin afghan

This design is one of the most popular for both quilts and afghans, and while it looks complicated, it is one of the easiest projects to crochet. Each square is made individually with a border around the block. Then the squares are all stitched together. This makes it easy to take your work with you for spare moments.

The wide range of yarn colors that can be used makes this design even more desirable, as you can follow the directions with your own color combination. The finished project is 54×76 inches.

Materials: Phildar Leader 3½-oz. skeins—5 skeins off white (color A—#30 Stone white), 5 skeins gold (color D—#44), 3 skeins yellow (color B—#89 Saffron), 8 skeins rust (color E—#50 horsechestnut), 9 skeins of dark brown (color C—#92), 3 skeins light brown (color F—#15 Buffalo).

Hook: #H
Gauge: Each square is 12 inches

Directions

Refer to diagram for color chart.
Center: With A (white), ch 15.
Row 1: 1 sc in 3rd ch from hook; (ch 1, sk 1 ch, 1 sc in next ch) 6 times.
Row 2: Ch 2, turn. 1 sc in 1st ch 1 sp; (ch 1, 1 sc in next ch 1 sp) 5 times; ch 1, 1 sc in sp under ch 2 at end of row.
Rows 3 through 14: Repeat row 2 twelve times.
At end of row 14, change to color B (yellow) in last sc.
To change colors: Work last sc of row until there are 2 loops on hook. Leave 4-inch ends and finish off color being used. With new color, yo and draw through 2 loops on hook. You now have a color change.

B band
Row 1: Ch 2, turn; working back across row just worked, 1 sc in 1st ch 1 sp; (ch 1, 1 sc in next ch 1 sp) 5 times; ch 1, work (1 sc, ch 2, 1 sc) in ch 2 sp at end of row for corner.
Continuing across side edge of white (A) center, work (ch 1, sk next row, 1 sc in next row) 6 times; ch 1, sk last row, 1 sc in beg ch of foundation chain.
Row 2: Ch 2, turn; work (1 sc, ch 1) in each ch 1 sp to ch 2 sp at corner; work (1 sc, ch 2, 1 sc) in corner sp.

Work (ch 1, 1 sc) in each ch 1 sp across, ending ch 1, 1 sc in sp under turning ch.
Rows 3 through 7: Repeat row 2 five times. At end of row 7, change to color C (dark brown) in last sc.

C band
Row 1: Ch 2, do not turn. Working across ends of B (yellow) rows and along beg row of white center, (1 sc in next row, ch 1, sk next row) 3 times; 1 sc in 1st sc of white center; (ch 1, 1 sc in next ch 1 sp) 6 times. Ch 1, work (1 sc, ch 2, 1 sc) in ch 2 sp at corner. Working across side edge of white center and ends of B (yellow) band, (ch 1, 1sc in next row, sk next row) 6 times; (ch 1, 1 sc in next row) twice (1 row of each color); (ch 1, sk next row, 1 sc in next row) 3 times.
Rows 2 through 7: Repeat rows 2 through 7 of B band (yellow). At end of row 7, change to D (gold) in last sc.

D band: On first row, you will be working across ends of C band (dark brown).
Row 1: Ch 2, do not turn; (1 sc in next row, ch 1, sk next row) 3 times; ch 1, 1 sc in turning ch sp at beg of next color band.
Work (ch 1, 1 sc in next ch 1 sp) in each ch 1 sp to corner; ch 1, work (1 sc, ch 2, 1 sc) in corner sp; work (ch 1, 1 sc in next ch 1 sp) in each ch 1 sp to beg of next color band; ch 1, 1 sc in 1st row (at end of next color band); (ch 1, sk next row, 1 sc in next row) 3 times.
Rows 2 through 7: Repeat rows 2 through 7 of B (yellow) band. At end of row 7, change to E (rust) in last sc.

E band: On first row you will be working across ends of D band (gold), and along last row of C band (dark brown). Work same as D band (gold). At end of last row, change to F (light brown) color in last sc.

F band: On first row, you will be working across ends of E band (rust) and along last row of D band (gold). At end of last row, change to C (dark brown) in last sc.

C band: On first row, you will be working across ends of F band (light brown) and along last row of E band (rust). Work same as D band (yellow). At end of last row, finish off.
Make 20 blocks.

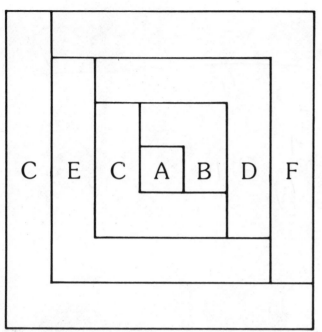

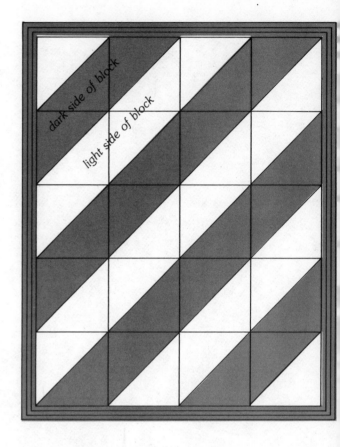

A—white
B—yellow
C—dark brown

D—saffron (gold)
E—horsechestnut (rust)
F—buffalo (gray)

Border around squares: With A (white) color, ch 1, sk 1 ch, 2 sc in corner and continue to sc 1 row around each block. Follow diagram and arrange squares as shown. To join, hold 2 squares with right sides tog, and sew or sc blocks together, with 4 squares across and 5 squares down. Join the squares in rows and then join rows.

Edging: With right sides facing, join D color (gold) with sl st in any outer corner sp of afghan.

Rnd 1: Ch 1, work (1 sc, ch 2, 1 sc, ch 1) in same sp; work (1 sc, ch 1) in each ch sp of squares outside borders, and in each remaining corner sp work (1 sc, ch 2, 1 sc, ch 1). Join with sl st in beg sc.

Rnd 2: Ch 1, turn; sl st into ch 1 sp, ch 1; 1 sc in same sp, ch 1. Work (1 sc, ch 1) in each ch 1 sp around. In each corner sp work (1 sc, ch 2, 1 sc, ch 1). Join with a sl st in beg sc.

Repeat rnd 2 twice more. At end of rnd 4 finish off D color (gold).

Rnd 5: Turn and join E color (rust) with a sl st in any corner space. Ch 1, (1 sc, ch 2, 1 sc, ch 1) in same space. Complete rnd in same manner as rnd 2.

Rnds 6 through 8: Repeat rnd 2 three times. At end of rnd 8, finish off E (rust).

Rnd 9: With C (dark brown), repeat rnd 5.

Rnds 10 through 12: Repeat rnd 2 three times. At end of rnd 12 finish off.

Finish: Weave in all ends, and block if necessary around border.

Winter baby socks p. 60

Doggy mittens p. 40

Christmas scarf p. 28

Teddy bear p. 53

Cable sleeve knit p. 58

Classic his or her knit p. 56

Striped carryall p. 92

Daisy pillow p. 118

Carriage blanket and pillow p. 88

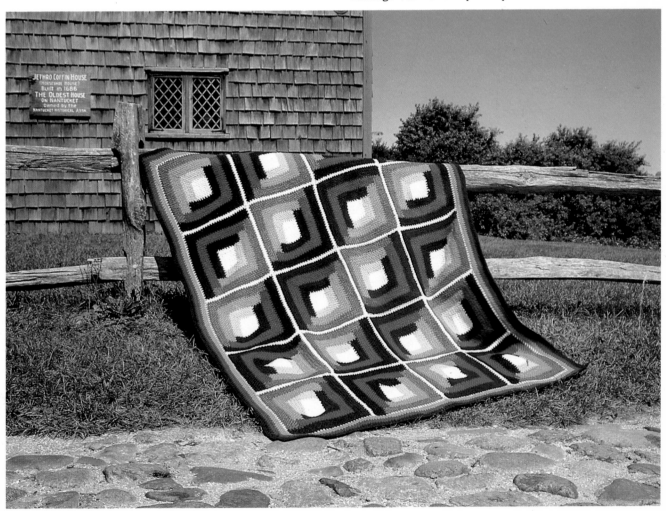

Log cabin afghan p. 126

Christmas basket p. 143

Ribbon sweater p. 46

Chelsea sweater set p. 64

Knit edgings p. 51

Guest towel edgings p. 113

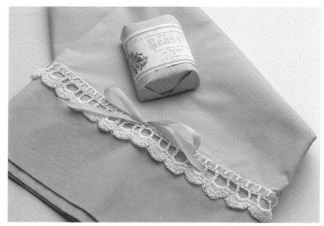

Pillowcase trim p. 111

Crocheted bag p. 104

Napkin edging p. 110

Crocheted doily p. 96

Christmas doily p. 98

Granny square place mat p. 78

Tote bag p. 124

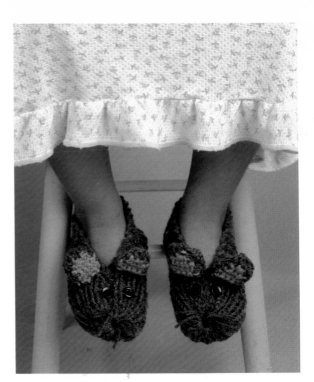

Mouse slippers p. 36

Three mouseketeers p. 146

Crocheted medallion pillow p. 100

Pineapple basket p. 135

Infant sweater p. 67

Soft baby blanket p. 48

Crocheted beach bag p. 120

Knit cap p. 44

Sport sweater p. 30

Simple blouson sweater p. 26

Scrap yarn cap p. 80

This and the following crochet projects come from Sally V. George of Baker, Oregon. I think you will find her patterns easy to follow and fun to make. The source list at the end of the book will tell you how to get in touch with Sally for more patterns.

Everyone loves rainbows, and this swinging mobile with its colorful combination of yarns will cheer someone in the hospital or entertain baby for hours. You can hang it in a window or allow it to swing freely. If everyone contributes leftover yarn, you can even make it in quantity for bazaar sales.

Materials: Acrylic 4-ply knitting worsted weight—1 oz. white; ½ oz each of pale yellow, bright yellow, and orange; a few yards each of purple, blue, green, red and black; polyester fiberfill; yarn needle; 7–8-inch plastic lid (large margarine tub) or similar plastic (sides of large bleach container or plastic needlepoint canvas).

Hook: #G

Gauge: 4 sc = 1 inch

       4 rows sc = 1 inch

Directions

The overall height of the mobile is 20 inches. You will make the rainbow in one piece, which you fold in half.

Starting at bottom of arc, with purple, ch 30, being careful not to twist ch, join with a sl st to form a circle, ch 1.

Note: When working rounds in sc that are joined with a sl st, Sally always works the first sc into the same sc that is sl st into (also called the joining st). That way all the sl sts line up on top of each other and are not counted or worked into.

Rnd 1: * Sc in each of next 4 ch, 2 sc in next ch, (sc in each of next 2 ch, 2 sc in next ch) twice, sc in each of next 4 ch **; ch 1, rep from * to ** once, join, ch 1 (36 sc).

Rnd 2: * Sc in each of next 5 sc, 2 sc in next sc, (sc in each of next sc, 2 sc in next sc) twice, sc in each of next 4 sc**; ch 1, rep from * to ** once, join. End off purple (42 sc).

Note: To attach new colors, insert hook between front and back loops of joining st of last rnd made. Draw up a loop of new color, then ch 1 and proceed as directed. To avoid weaving in yarn ends, place

them across top of rnd and work new stitches over them.

Rnd 3: With blue, in back lps only, * sc in each of next 4 sc, 2 sc in next sc, (sc in each of next 3 sc, 2 sc in next sc) 3 times, sc in each of next 4 sc **; ch 1, rep from * to ** once, join, ch 1 (50 sc).

Rnd 4: * Sc in each of next 6 sc, (sc in each of next 5 sc, 2 sc in next sc) twice, sc in each of next 6 sc **; ch 1, rep from * to ** once, join. End off blue (56 sc).

Rnd 5: With green, in back lps only, * sc in each of next 5 sc, 2 sc in next sc, sc in each of next 4 sc, 2 sc in next sc, sc in each of next 6 sc, 2 sc in next sc, sc in each of next 4 sc, 2 sc in next sc, sc in each of next 5 sc**; ch 1, rep from * to ** once, join, ch 1 (64 sc).

Rnd 6: Sc in each of next 8 sc, 2 sc in next sc, (sc in each of next 6 sc, 2 sc in next sc) twice, sc in each of next 9 sc**; ch 1, rep from * to ** once, join. End off green (70 sc).

Rnd 7: With yellow, in back lps only, * sc in each of next 13 sc, 2 sc in next sc, sc in each of next 7 sc, 2 sc in next sc, sc in each of next 13 sc**; ch 1, rep from * to ** once, join, ch 1 (74 sc).

Rnd 8: * Sc in each of the next 37 sc**; ch 1, rep from * to ** once, join. End off yellow (74 sc).

Rnd 9: With orange, in back lps only, * sc in each of next 10 sc, 2 sc in next sc, (sc in each of next 7 sc, 2 sc in next sc) twice, sc in each of next 10 sc**; ch 1, rep from * to ** once, join, ch 1 (80 sc).

Rnd 10: * Sc in each of next 14 sc, 2 sc in next sc, sc in each of next 10 sc, 2 sc in next sc, sc in each of next 14 sc**; ch 1, rep from * to ** once, join. End off orange (84 sc).

Rnd 11: With red, in back lps only, * sc in each of next 12 sc, 2 sc in next sc, (sc in each of next 8 sc, 2 sc in next sc) twice, sc in each of next 11 sc**; ch 1, rep from * to ** once, join, ch 1 (90 sc). Do not cut yarn.

Rnd 12: Fold rainbow along rows of ch 1. Cut ridged lip off plastic lid. Cut lid (or whatever type of plastic you have) to fit inside folded rainbow. It may take a few tries with an extra snip here and there. Don't worry if it doesn't come down completely in the corners. Put the plastic inside the folded rainbow. Working through both layers, under both loops of each st, sc in each of next 10 sc, 2 sc in next sc, (sc in each of next 7 sc, 2 sc in next sc) 3 times, sc in each of next 10 sc. End off (49 sc). With some purple yarn on a needle, stitch the purple edges together.

Cloud

Side 1: Starting in center, with white, ch 2.
Rnd 1: 10 sc in 1st ch; do not join with sl st, but work in a continuous spiral, marking the beg of each rnd with a length of contrasting-color yarn, which you carry up each rnd.
Rnd 2: 2 sc in each sc (20 sc).
Rnd 3: (Sc in each of next 2 sc, 2 sc in next sc) 6 times, sc in each of last 2 sc (26 sc).
Rnd 4: Sc in each sc (26 sc).
Rnd 5: (2 sc in next sc, sc in each of next 2 sc) 8 times, 2 sc in next sc, sc in last sc (35 sc).
Rnd 6: Sk next sc, 4 dc in next sc, dc in next sc, 2 dc in each of next 2 sc, 1 hdc in next sc, (2 sc in next sc, sc in each of next 2 sc) 4 times, dc in next sc, 3 dc in next sc, 2 dc in next sc, dc in next sc, 1 hdc in next sc, sl st in next sc, ch 1, turn, (1 sc, 1 dc) in hdc, 3 dc in next dc, sc in each of next 2 dc, 2 sc in each of next 2 dc, sl st in next dc. End off.
Rnd 7: (To finish puff on other end of cloud) Insert hook in 4th dc made at beg of rnd 6, draw loop through, ch 2, dc in each of next 3 dc, 5 dc in next dc, sk next dc, sc in hdc, sl st in next sc, sc in each of next 14 sc, sl st in next sc, cut yarn, pull end through sl st just made, then pull yarn to back of work, going under back lp of next st (which is a dc).
Rnd 8: Now go back to beg of rnd 7, insert hook in first dc made after ch 2, draw lp through, ch 1, sk next dc, 5 dc in next dc, sl st in next dc to end off.

Side 2: Work the same as side 1 through rnd 4.
Rnd 5: (2 sc in next sc, sc in each of next 2 sc) 7 times, 2 sc in next sc, sc in next sc, 2 dc in each of next 2 sc, dc in next sc.
Rnd 6: 4 dc in next sc, sk next sc, sc in each of next 5 sc, 2 sc in next sc, sc in each of next 4 sc, hdc in next sc, 2 dc in next sc, 3 dc in next sc, dc in next sc, sc in each of next 2 sc, 2 sc in next sc, sc in each of next 3 sc, 2 sc in next sc, sc in each of next 7 sc, sl st in next sc, sc in dc, sk next dc, 5 dc in next dc, dc in each of next 2 dc. Keeping lps on hook, work 1 dc in each of next 2 dc (3 lps on hook), yo and through all 3 lps on hook; turn, sk one dc, 5 dc in next dc, end off with a sl st in next dc.

Rnd 7: (To finish puff at other end of cloud) Insert hook in hdc made at unfinished end of cloud, draw a lp through ch 1, (1 sc, 1 dc) in next dc, 3 dc in next dc, sc in each of next 2 dc, 2 sc in each of next 2 dc, sl st in next dc. End off.

Assembling cloud: Place wrong sides of cloud pieces together and sl st edges together with hook, going through both pieces and under both lps of each st. Or you can use a needle and lace the edges together, again going under both lps of each st. "Because each piece has been made slightly differently, don't worry if all the edges don't match stitch for stitch," says Sally. "Just ease the pieces together, taking long, easy slip stitches. Before you close it up altogether, add as much fiberfill stuffing as desired."

Sun

Center: Make 2. Beginning in the center, with bright yellow, ch 2.
Rnd 1: 8 sc in 1st ch. Do not join with sl st, but work in a continuous spiral, marking beg of each rnd with contrasting-color yarn.
Rnd 2: 2 sc in each sc (16 sc).
Rnd 3: (Sc in next sc, 2 sc in next sc) 8 times (24 sc).
Rnd 4: (Sc in each of next 3 sc, 2 sc in next sc) 6 times (30 sc).
Rnd 5: Sc in each sc.
Rnd 6: (2 sc in next sc, sc in ech of next 2 sc) 10 times. Sl st in each of next 2 sc, cut yarn and pull yarn end through last sl st and then down between front and back lp of next sc, making a nice smooth, tapered edge (38 sc and 2 sl sts).

Points of Sun's Rays: Place 2 yellow circles wrong sides together, with tapered ends of rnd 6 meeting each other. With orange, working through both pieces and under top lps only, insert hook in any sc on the edges. Pull lp through, ch 1, * sk next sc, 3 dc in next sc, ch 2, sl st in top of last dc made, 2 dc in same sc with other dc, sk next sc, sl st in next sc, *making pointed shell*. Rep from * around, working under top lps of edge sl sts when they come around. Stuff the center lightly with fiberfill before ending off (10 points).

Face: To make the eyes, use black 4-ply yarn for 2 French knots. To make the mouth, untwist some bright orange or red 4-ply to get 2-ply. Backstitch along the curve of the round. Satin stitch small cheeks at each end of smile.

Star

Side 1: Starting in center, with light yellow ch 4; join to form ring.

Rnd 1: Ch 1, 10 sc into center of ring, join.

Rnd 2: Ch 5, sc in 3rd ch from hook, sc in each of next 2 ch, sk joining st and next sc, sc in next sc, (ch 5, sc in 3rd ch from hook, sc in each of next 2 ch, sk next sc, sc in next sc) 4 times. Do not join (5 spokes).

Rnd 3: Ch 1; * working up side of spoke, sk first ch, sc in each of next 2 ch, (1 sc, ch 2, 1 sc) in tip of spoke, sc in each of next 2 sc on other side of spoke, sk next sc, hdc in next sc (between base of spokes), rep from * 4 times, joining into the ch 1 without making a hdc at the end of the rnd. End off.

Side 2: Starting in center, with light yellow, ch 4, join to form ring.

Rnd 1: Ch 1, 10 sc into center of ring, join.

Rnd 2: Ch 5, sc in 3rd ch from hook, sc in each of next 2 ch, sk joining st and next sc, sc in next sc, (ch 5, sc in 3rd ch from hook, sc in each of next 2 ch, sk next sc, sc in next sc) 4 times, working off last lp of last sc with bright yellow. End off the light yellow. Do not join.

Rnd 3: Continuing with bright yellow, ch 1, * working up side of spoke, sk first ch, sc in each of next 2 ch, (1 sc, ch 2, 1 sc) in tip of spoke, sc in each of next 2 sc on other side of spoke, sk next sc, hdc in next sc (between spokes), rep from * 4 times, join with a sl st in back lp of ch 1 without making a 5th hdc. Do not end off.

Place side 1, with wrong side facing you, behind side 2, matching points. Sl st under top lp of st on side 1 directly behind your hook. Ch 1, turn both pieces over so side 1 is toward you. Continue to next rnd.

Rnd 4: Working through both pieces and under top lps only, (sl st in each of next 3 sc, sl st in ch, ch 2, sl st in next ch, sl st in each of next 3 sc, sk hdc) 5 times, adding a small amount of stuffing before closing up. Join and end off.

Moon

Made in one piece, which you fold in half. Starting in the center at the tip of the nose, with light yellow, ch 2.

Rnd 1: 5 sc in lst ch, join, ch 1 (5 sc).

Rnd 2: Sc in each of the next 2 sc, 2 sc in next sc, sc in each of next 2 sc, join, ch 1 (6 sc).

Rnd 3: Sc in each of next 2 sc, 2 sc in each of next 2 sc, sc in each of next 2 sc, join, ch 1 (8 sc).

Rnd 4: Sc in each of next 2 sc, 2 sc in next sc, sc in each of next 2 sc, 2 sc in next sc, sc in each of next 2 sc, join, ch 1 (10 sc).

Rnd 5: Work (1 sc, 1 dc) in next sc, dc in next sc, sc in each of next 3 sc, 2 sc in next sc, sc in each of next 2 sc, dc in next sc, work (1 dc, 1 sc) in next sc, join, ch 1 (13 sts).

Rnd 6: 2 sc in next sc, sc in each of the next 2 dc, sc in each of next 2 sc, 2 sc in next sc, sc in next sc, 2 sc in next sc, sc in each of next 2 sc, sc in each of next 2 dc, 2 sc in next sc, join, ch 1 (17 sc).

Rnd 7: 2 sc in each of the next 2 sc, sc in each of the next 5 sc, 2 sc in next sc, sc in next sc, 2 sc in next sc, sc in each of next 5 sc, 2 sc in each of next 2 sc, join, ch 1 (23 sc).

Rnd 8: 2 sc in each of next 2 sc, sc in each of next 8 sc, 2 sc in next sc, sc in next sc, 2 sc in next sc, 1 sc in each of next 8 sc, 2 sc in each of next 2 sc, join, ch 1 (29 sc).

Rnd 9: 2 sc in next sc, sc in next sc, 2 sc in next sc, (sc in each of next 5 sc, 2 sc in next sc) 4 times, sc in next sc, 2 sc in next sc, join, ch 1 (36 sc).

Rnd 10: (2 sc in next sc, sc in each of next 6 sc) twice, 2 sc in next sc, sc in next sc, 2 sc in next sc, sc in each of next 2 sc, 2 sc in next sc, sc in next sc, (2 sc in next sc, sc in each of next 6 sc) twice, 2 sc in next sc, join, ch 1 (44 sc).

Rnd 11: (2 sc in next sc, sc in each of next 5 sc) twice, 2 sc in next sc, sc in each of next 8 sc, 2 sc in each of next 2 sc, sc in each of next 8 sc, 2 sc in next sc, (sc in each of next 5 sc, 2 sc in next sc) twice, join (52 sc).

Fold piece in half along joining sts at the bottom, which will automatically fold the top part above the nose. Put just a small bit of stuffing in nose and center of face.

Rnd 12: Ch 3, sc in lst ch from hook, sc in next ch, sc in joining st, then, working through both pieces and under both lps, sc in next sc, 2 sc in next sc, sc in each of next 4 sc, 2 sc in next sc, sc in each of next 16 sc, 2 sc in each of next 2 sc, ch 3, sc in lst ch from hook, sc in next ch, sl st into sc on the fold. Cut yarn, pull end through loop on hook and then through same st to the inside and weave in.

Face: Untwist some orange 4-ply to get 2-ply and use this for eyes and mouth. For eyes, take one long straight stitch to make a lid, outline stitch the lashes. Use a backstitch along the curve between rnds 8 and 9 for the mouth. Work from one side of the face to the other, but not through 2 layers at once.

Assembly: Attach red yarn to top center of rainbow and make a chain as long as you want to reach your hanging hook; sl st into 8th ch from hook and each of next 5 ch to form a hanging loop. Weave yarn end through ch. Cut the following lengths of yarn:
8 inches of bright yellow for star
12 inches of pale yellow for moon
19 inches of white for cloud
10 inches of bright yellow for sun.
Tie one end of each length of yarn to its appropriate item. Following photograph for placement, tie each item loosely to rainbow, allowing a 1-inch drop for star; a 5-inch drop for moon; an 11¾-inch drop for cloud; and a 3-inch drop for sun. Check balance before tightening knots, and weave all yarn ends into rainbow and each item. However, if you have varied yarn at all, you may have to shorten or lengthen some drops to get a good balance.

Pineapple lace basket

There is nothing prettier than a delicately lacy basket made of fine crochet. While this project isn't really quick and easy, it is worth the time and effort.

You can make the two sizes shown from the same pattern. For the larger basket you simply use a larger bottle around which to make the form, which will stretch to this size.

Materials: Coats & Clark's Knit-Cro-Sheen, approximately 100 yards; plastic 2-liter soft drink bottle or 28-oz. peanut butter jar; sheet of Styrofoam approximately 1x12 inches; plastic wrap; stainless steel pins; starch or Stif 'n Fab.
Hook: Steel #6
Gauge: 8 dc = 1 inch
    4 rows dc = 1 inch

Directions

Beginning at center bottom, ch 4, join with sl st to form ring.
Rnd 1: Ch 3 (counts as 1 dc in this and all following rnds), work 11 dc into ring, join in top of ch 3 (12 dc).
Rnd 2: Ch 3, dc in same st, ch 1, * 2 dc in next dc, ch 1, rep from * around, join as before (24 dc; 12 sp).
Rnd 3: Ch 3, dc in next dc, ch 1, * dc in each of next 2 dc, ch 1, rep from * around, join (24 dc, 12 sp).
Rnd 4: Ch 3, dc in next dc, ch 2, * dc in each of next 2 dc, ch 2, rep from * around, join (24 dc, 12 sp).
Rnd 5: Ch 3, 2 dc in next dc, ch 2, * dc in next dc, 2 dc in next dc, ch 2, rep from * around, join (36 dc, 12 sp).
Rnd 6: Ch 3, dc in each of next 2 dc, ch 3, * dc in each of next 3 dc, ch 3, rep from * around, join (36 dc, 12 sp).
Rnd 7: Ch 3, dc in next dc, 2 dc in next dc, ch 3, * dc in each of next 2 dc, 2 dc in next dc, ch 3, rep from * around, join (48 dc, 12 sp).
Next 3 Rnds (8, 9, 10): Ch 3, dc in each of next 3 dc, ch 4, * dc in each of next 4 dc, ch 4, rep from * around, join (12 groups of 4 dc, 12 sp).
Rnd 11: Sl st in each of next 2 dc, (ch 3, 1 dc, ch 1, 2 dc) in next st, ch 3; (2 dc, ch 1, 2 dc) in 3rd dc of next group of 4 dc, *making shell*, ch 3, * 9 dc in 3rd dc of next group of 4, dc *beginning pineapple*, ch 3, (shell in 3rd dc of next group of 4 dc, ch 3) twice, repeat from * around, ending with ch 3 after 9 dc, join (4 pineapples, 8 shells).

Rnd 12: Sl st across top of shell to ch 3 sp, (ch 3, 1 dc, ch 1, 2 dc) in ch 3 sp, * sk shell, ch 4, (1 dc, ch 1) in each of next 8 dc, dc in 9th dc, ch 4, shell in ch 3 sp between next 2 shells, rep from * around, ending with ch 4 after pineapple, join (4 pineapples, 4 shells).
Rnd 13: Sl st across to ch 1 sp, (ch 3, 1 dc, ch 1, 2 dc) in sp, * (ch 4, 1 sc) in each of 8 ch 1 sps between dc's, ch 4, shell in shell, rep from * around, ending with ch 4, join.
Rnd 14: Sl st across to ch 1 sp, (ch 3, 1 dc, ch 1, 2 dc) in sp, * (ch 4, 1 sc) in each of 7 ch 4 loops across pineapple, ch 4, shell in shell, repeat from * around, ending with ch 4, join.
Rnd 15: Repeat rnd 14, having 1 less ch 4 loop across each pineapple. There should be 5 loops on each pineapple at end of round.
Rnd 16: Sl st to ch 1 sp, ch 3, 1 dc in sp, (ch 1, 2 dc) twice in same sp with other dc, *making a shell with 3 groups of 2 dc and 2 sps,* * (ch 4, 1 sc) in each of 5 ch 4 loops, ch 4, (2 dc, ch 1, 2 dc, ch 1, 2 dc) in next shell, rep from * around, ending with ch 4, join.
Rnd 17: Sl st to lst ch 1 sp, (ch 3, 1 dc, ch 1, 2 dc) in sp, * ch 1, shell in next ch 1 sp, (ch 4, 1 sc) in each of 4 ch 4 loops, ch 4, shell in next ch 1 sp, rep from * around, ending with ch 4, join (4 pineapples, 8 shells).
Rnd 18: Sl st to lst ch 1 sp, (ch 3, 1 dc, ch 1, 2 dc) in sp, * ch 1, shell in ch 1 sp between shells, ch 1, shell in shell, (ch 4, 1 sc) in each of 3 ch 4 loops, ch 4, shell in next shell, rep from * around, ending with ch 4, join (4 pineapples, 12 shells).
Rnd 19: Sl st to 1st ch 1 sp, (ch 3, 1 dc, ch 1, 2 dc) all in same sp, * (ch 3, shell in shell) twice, (ch 4, 1 sc) in each of 2 ch 4 lp (leaving only one lp at top of pineapple), ch 4, shell in shell, repeat from * around, ending with ch 4, join.
Rnd 20: Sl st to lst ch 1 sp, (ch 3, 1 dc, ch 1, 2 dc) in sp, * (ch 4, shell in shell) twice, ch 4, sc in last ch 4 lp of pineapple, ch 4, shell in shell, repeat from * around, ending with ch 4, join (12 shells).
Rnd 21: Sl st to lst ch 1 sp, (ch 3, 1 dc, ch 1, 2 dc) in sp, * (ch 5, shell in shell) twice, ch 1, shell in shell, repeat from * around, ending with ch 1, join.
Rnd 22: Sl st to lst ch 1 sp, (ch 3, 1 dc) in sp, * ch 6, shell in shell, ch 6, 2 dc in next shell, ch 1, 2 dc in next shell, *making new shell,* repeat from * around, ending with 2 dc, ch 1, join, *making another new shell* (8 shells).
Rnd 23: Ch 7 (counts as 1 dc and 4 ch), * (1 dc, ch 1)

4 times, 1 dc, all in next shell; ch 4, rep from * around, ending with (1 dc, ch 1) 4 times in last shell, join in 3rd ch of ch 7.

Rnd 24: Sl st into ch 4 sp, (ch 8, 1 sc) twice in same sp, * (ch 8, 1 sc) in each ch 1 sp between dc, (ch 8, 1 sc) 3 times in next ch 4 sp, repeat from * around, ending with ch 4, 1 tr in sl st made at beg of rnd (56 loops).

Next 3 rnds (25, 26, 27): (Ch 8, 1 sc) in each ch 8 loop around, ending with ch 4, 1 tr in tr except on last rnd, when a ch 8, 1 sc in tr will work. End off.

Handle

Ch 8, (1 dc, ch 1, 2 dc) in 4th ch from hook, *making shell;* sk next 3 ch, (2 dc, ch 1, 2 dc) in last ch, making *another shell.*

Next 40 rows: Ch 3, turn, shell in each of 2 shells. End off.

Starching: If using the 2-liter plastic bottle, stretch basket over the bottom and pull up as high as possible. Mark bottle approximately ¼ inch above rnd 23, (last rnd before ruffle begins). Remove basket from bottle and cut all around bottle at mark. Discard top.

Cover sheet of Styrofoam with plastic wrap. Soak basket and handle in Stif 'n Fab or heavy starch solution (made as directed on package). Squeeze out excess liquid.

Slip basket over bottle or peanut butter jar. Turn upside down onto Styrofoam sheet and pin rnd 23 to board. Using your fingers, stretch ruffle out all around and shape it into ripples. No pinning is necessary.

When outer edges of ruffles begin to dry, but before rnd 23 is thoroughly dry, remove pins.

Set bottle or jar, still upside down, over something taller, like a can or iced tea drinking glass, to let ruffle hang down to finish drying. In the meantime, lay handle out flat. Stretch, pin and let dry.

When both pieces are completely dry, remove basket from jar or bottle (loosen with dinner knife), unpin handle and sew handle inside basket. For an added touch, weave a narrow ribbon through handle and tie a bow at top.

The emergency "candle" in this case is a well-concealed flashlight hidden inside a potato chip can with a crocheted covering. Sally George gives her friend Becky Leshley credit for this clever idea, which I think you'll agree is one worth trying.

Materials: Acrylic 4-ply knitting worsted weight yarn, 2 oz. gold or color of your choice for candlestick, 1½ oz. yarn for candle (white used here), a few yards yellow for flame, empty Pringle's can with lid.
Hook: #G
Gauge: 4 sc = 1 inch
4 rows sc = 1 inch

Directions

Candlestick

Starting at top center, ch 36; being careful not to twist ch, join with sl st to make circle, ch 1.

When working rounds in sc that are joined with a sl st, work the first sc into the same sc that sl st is in (also called the joining st). In this way all the sl sts line up on top of each other and are not counted or worked into.

Rnd 1: (1 sc in each of next 3 ch, 2 sc in next ch) 9 times, join with sl st, ch 1 (45 sc).

Rnd 2: (1 sc in each of next 4 sc, 2 sc in next sc) 9 times, *completing top of drip lip*, join, ch 1 (54 sc).

Rnd 3: Working in back loops only, 1 sc in each sc, *making edge of lip*, join, ch 1 (54 sc).

Rnd 4: Working in back lps only, (1 sc in each of next 5 sc, sk next sc) 9 times, join, ch 1 (45 sc).

Rnd 5: (1 sc in each of next 4 sc, sk next sc) 9 times, *completing underside of lip*, join, ch 1 (36 sc).

Rnd 6: Working in front lps only, 1 sc in each, join, ch 1 (36 sc).

Next 3 rnds (7, 8, 9): 1 sc in each sc, join, ch 1 (36 sc).

Rnd 10: Turn; working in back lps only, 1 sc in sl st and each of next 4 sc, 2 sc in next sc, (1 sc in each of next 5 sc, 2 sc in next sc) 5 times, join, ch 1 (42 sc).

Rnd 11: (1 sc in each of next 5 sc, dec next 2 sc) 6 times, join, ch 1 (36 sc).

Rnd 12: Turn. Insert hook in back lp of sl st. Take a moment now to look inside tube and locate free lps left unworked on rnd 10. Push your hook down so it slips under 1st free lp of rnd 10, which is a sl st also (check on outside of your work to be sure you have

right stitch); yo, draw lp through 1st 2 loops on hook, yo and through last 2 loops, completing sc. Continuing in this manner, working in back lps only of two rnds as one, sc in each of next 35 sc, join, ch 1 (36 sc).

Rnd 13: 1 sc in each sc, join, ch 1 (36 sc).

Rnd 14: (beginning saucer) working in front lps only, (1 sc in each of next 5 sc, 2 sc in next sc) 6 times, join, ch 1 (42 sc).

Rnd 15: 1 sc in each of next 3 sc, 2 sc in next sc, (1 sc in each of next 6 sc, 2 sc in next sc) 5 times, 1 sc in each of last 3 sc, join, ch 1 (48 sc).

Rnd 16: (1 sc in each of next 5 sc, 2 sc in next sc) 8 times, join, ch 1 (56 sc).

Rnd 17: 1 sc in each of next 3 sc, 2 sc in next sc, (1 sc in each of next 6 sc, 2 sc in next sc) 7 times, 1 sc in each of last 3 sc, join, ch 1 (64 sc).

Rnd 18: (1 sc in each of next 7 sc, 2 sc in next sc) 8 times, join, ch 1 (72 sc).

Rnd 19: 1 sc in each sc, join, ch 1 (72 sc).

Rnd 20: 1 sc in each of next 4 sc, 2 sc in next sc, (1 sc in each of next 8 sc, 2 sc in next sc) 7 times, 1 sc in each of last 4 sc, join, ch 1 (80 sc).

Rnd 21: 1 sc in each sc, *completing top of saucer*, join, ch 1 (80 sc).

Rnd 22: Working in back lps only, 1 sc in each sc, *making edge of saucer*, join, ch 1 (80 sc).

Rnd 23: Working in back lps only, 1 sc in each sc, join, ch 1 (80 sc).

Rnd 24: 1 sc in each sc, join, ch 1 (80 sc).

Rnd 25: 1 sc in each of next 5 sc, sk next sc, (1 sc in each of next 9 sc, sk next sc) 7 times, 1 sc in each of last 4 sc, join, ch 1 (72 sc).

Rnd 26: (1 sc in each of next 8 sc, sk next sc) 8 times, join, ch 1 (64 sc).

Rnd 27: 1 sc in each of next 4 sc, sk next sc, (1 sc in each of next 7 sc, sk next sc) 7 times, 1 sc in each of next 3 sc, join, ch 1 (56 sc).

Rnd 28: (1 sc in each of next 6 sc, sk next sc) 8 times, join, ch 1 (48 sc).

Rnd 29: 1 sc in each of next 3 sc, sk next sc, (1 sc in each of next 7 sc, sk next sc) 5 times, 1 sc in each of last 4 sc, join, ch 1 (42 sc).

Rnd 30: (1 sc in each of next 6 sc, sk next sc) 6 times, join, ch 1 (36 sc).

Rnd 31: 1 sc in each sc, *completing underside of saucer*, join (36 sc). End off, leaving 12 inches yarn for sewing. Press underside of saucer close up under top of saucer, and sew rnd 31 to inside of tube, taking needle under back lps only of rnd 31 and free lps only of rnd 14. Do not sew top lip together yet.

Handle

Make 2. Ch 8, join with sl st to form ring, ch 1; work 23 sc in ring, pushing sts close together, completely covering ch, join. End off.

Place rings back to back; working through both pieces as one and placing hook under both loops of each sc, sl st in each sc around, join. End off, leaving 8 inches yarn for sewing. Place ring in saucer so it covers joining sts made at ends of rnds. Sew edges of ring to side of candlestick and along curve of saucer as shown in photo.

Candle

Lift top lip up and outward, folding it down around outside of candlestick. This will allow you to see free lps left unworked on rnd 6. Holding outside of piece toward you, insert hook under back loop of joining st on this rnd (rnd 6) and draw through a loop of color chosen for candle; ch 1.

Rnd 1: 1 sc in each free loop around (36 sc). Do not join with sl st, but work in continuous spiral, marking beg of each rnd with a contrasting-color strand of yarn which you carry up each rnd.

Next 27 rnds: 1 sc in each sc.

Rnd 29: 1 sc in each of next 5 sc, sl st in next sc, ch 1, turn, leaving rest of rnd unworked.

Rnd 30: Sk sl st, 1 sc in each of next 21 sc, sl st in each of next 5 sc, ch 16, 3 sc in 2nd ch from hook, sl st back up ch, *making first drip of wax,* sl st in same sc where ch began, sl st in each of next 2 sc, ch 12, 3 sc in 2nd ch from hook, sl st back up the ch, *making 2nd drip,* sl st in same sc where ch began and each of next 5 sc, ch 8, 3 sc in 2nd ch from hook, sl st back up the ch, *making 3rd drip,* sl st in same sc where ch began, sl st in each of next 2 sc, and join with sl st in ch 1. End off.

Split a matching strand of 4-ply yarn to get two 2-ply strands. Use these to tack drips to sides of candle.

Candle flame

With yellow, ch 7; 2 sc in 2nd ch from hook, 1 hdc in each of next 3 ch, 1 sc in next ch, sl st in last ch, ch 2, sl st in 2nd ch from hook; working along opposite side of ch, lay beginning tail of yarn on top of ch and work over it; sl st in lst ch, 1 sc in next ch, 1 hdc in next ch, 2 dc in next ch, 1 dc in next ch, (1 hdc, 1 sc) in last ch, join to lst sc. End off, leaving 6 inches yarn for sewing.

Candletop

Starting at center, with color used for candle, ch 2.
Rnd 1: 6 sc in 2nd ch from hook. Do not join with sl st but work in continuous spiral, marking each rnd with a strand of contrasting-color yarn.
Rnd 2: 2 sc in each sc (12 sc).
Rnd 3: (2 sc in next sc, sc in next sc) 6 times (18 sc).
Rnd 4: (2 sc in next sc, sc in each of next 2 sc) 6 times (24 sc).
Rnd 5: (2 sc in next sc, sc in each of next 3 sc) 6 times (30 sc).
Rnd 6: (2 sc in next sc, sc in each of next 4 sc) 6 times (36 sc).
End off, leaving 15 inches yarn for sewing.

Assembly

Place flame in center of candletop and sew securely. Place candletop on open top of candle so flat edge of flame faces drips. Sew edges together taking needle under one loop only of each piece. Untwist strand of 4-ply yarn in color of candlestick to get two 2-ply strands. Pull drip lip back up to its original position at base of candle. Flatten top and underside of lip together. Sew 2 pieces together, taking needle up and down through both layers with easy stitches running along inside edge close to candle. Do not pull sts too tightly or you'll have "pit" marks.

Turn Pringle's can upside down. Slip candle and candlestick over can so lid of can is at bottom of candlestick. Take off lid—insert flashlight—replace lid. Shape edges of saucer with fingers so they curve up evenly all around.

Little airplane

This adorable toy airplane is soft and washable for babies who enjoy squeezing and chewing. Combine three planes and a cloud or two from the Rainbow Mobile (page 129) to make a hanging for over the crib.

Materials: Acrylic 4-ply knitting worsted weight yarn—1 oz. bright color for body and wings; a few yards dark color for wheels and propeller; polyfil stuffing.
Hook: #G or size needed to obtain gauge.
Gauge: 4 sc = 1 inch
        4 rows sc = 1 inch

Directions

The size of the finished project measures 5½ inches nose to tail. There is a 6-inch wing span.

Body
Starting at nose, ch 2.
Rnd 1: 6 sc in 1st ch. Do not join with a sl st, but work in continuous spiral, marking beg of each rnd with a strand of contrasting-color yarn which you carry up each rnd.
Rnd 2: 2 sc in each sc (12 sc).
Rnd 3: (1 sc in each of next 3 sc, 2 sc in next sc) 3 times (15 sc).
Rnd 4: (1 sc in ech of next 2 sc, 2 sc in next sc) 5 times (20 sc).
Rnd 5: (1 sc in each of next 3 sc, 2 sc in next sc) 5 times (25 sc).
Rnd 6: 1 sc in each sc (25 sc).
Rnd 7: Working in front lps only, 1 sc in each of next 2 sc, 2 dc in next sc, 1 dc in next sc, 2 dc in next sc, 1 sc in each of next 2 sc; working under both lps now, 1 sc in each of next 18 sc (27 sts).
Rnd 8: 1 sc in next sc, 2 sc in next sc; working in back lps only, 1 sc in each of next 2 dc, 2 sc in next dc, 1 sc in each of next 2 dc; working under both lps now, 2 sc in next sc, 1 sc in each of next 19 sc (30 sc).
Next 4 rnds: 1 sc in each sc (30 sc).
Rnd 13: (1 sc in each of next 3 sc, dec next 2 sc) twice, 1 sc in each of next 6 sc, dec next 2 sc, (1 sc in each of next 3 sc, dec next 2 sc) twice, 1 sc in each of last 2 sc (25 sc).

Rnd 14: 1 sc in each of next 2 sc, dec next 2 sc, 1 sc in each of next 4 sc, dec next 2 sc, 1 sc in each of next 15 sc (23 sc).
Rnd 15: 1 sc in each sc (23 sc).
Rnd 16: 1 sc in each of next 2 sc, dec next 2 sc, 1 sc in each of next 3 sc, dec next 2 sc, 1 sc in each of next 4 sc, (dec next 2 sc, 1 sc in next sc) twice, dec next 2 sc, 1 sc in each of last 2 sc (18 sc). Stuff firmly without stretching.
Rnd 17: 1 sc in first sc, dec next 2 sc, (1 sc in each of next 3 sc, dec next 2 sc) twice, 1 sc in next sc, dec next 2 sc, 1 sc in each of last 2 sc (14 sc).
Rnd 18: 1 sc in 1st sc, dec next 2 sc, 1 sc in each of next 2 sc, dec next 2 sc, 1 sc in each of next 7 sc (12 sc).
Rnd 19: 1 sc in each of next 2 sc, dec next 2 sc, 1 sc in each of next 4 sc, dec next 2 sc, 1 sc in each of last 2 sc (10 sc).
Rnd 20: Dec 1st 2 sc, (1 sc in next sc, dec next 2 sc) twice, dec last 2 sc. (6 sc) Poke in more stuffing to firm out tail end.
Flatten last 6 sc together, folding between last 2 dec sc so they are face to face and to your right. Working through both thicknesses as if they were one, 1 sc in each of the remaining 2 scs. Do not end off but continue on to tail.

Tail

Upright fin: Ch 6, 1 dc in 3rd ch from hook and each of next 2 ch, ch 1, turn; 1 sc in each of next 3 dc, 1 sc in ch, 2 sc in each of next 2 ch; working into free lps rem from ch 6, 1 sc in each of next 3 ch, 1 sc in next sc, sl st in last sc. End off, leaving 6 inches yarn for sewing. Lean this flap toward nose of plane so flat end of flap lies along top of body across rnds 18, 19 and 20. Sew in place.

Side fins: Make 2. Ch 5, 1 dc in 3rd ch from hook, 1 hdc in next ch, ch 1, turn; 1 sc in hdc, 1 sc in dc, 1 sc in ch, 2 sc in next ch, 1 sc in next ch; working into free lps remaining from ch 5, 1 sc in each of next 2 ch. End off, leaving 6 inches yarn for sewing. Place flat edges of each piece across rnds 18, 19 and 20, along sides of body level with yarn marking ends of the rnds—or imaginary line from tip of nose to tip of tail; sew securely.

Wings

Make 2. Starting at tip, ch 2.

Rnd 1: 6 sc in lst ch, join with sl st, ch 1.

Note: When working rounds in sc that are joined with a sl st, work the first sc into the same sc that sl st is in (also called the joining st). That way all sl sts line up on top of each other and are not counted or worked into.

Rnd 2: (2 sc in next sc, 1 sc in next sc, 2 sc in next sc) twice, join, ch 1 (10 sc).

Rnd 3: 1 sc in each of next 4 sc, 2 sc in next sc, 1 sc in each of next 5 sc, join, ch 1 (11 sc).

Next 3 rnds: 1 sc in each sc, join, ch 1.

Rnd 7: 1 sc in each of next 5 sc, 2 sc in next sc, 1 sc in each of next 5 sc, join, ch 1 (12 sc).

Rnd 8: 1 sc in each sc, join. End off, leaving 10 inches for sewing. Flatten piece with joining sts on one edge. This is the back of wing. Place wing on side of body with top of wing level with that imaginary line running from tip of nose to tip of tail. Place front edge 2 rnds behind windshield. Sew on securely, taking needle under front lps only of sts on the wings. *Note:* St through each of the 12 sc around. If you sew through both layers as one, the wing will flop.

Propeller

Starting at center, * ch 6, 1 sc in 2nd ch from hook, 1 dc in next ch, 1 hdc in next ch, sl st in last ch **; ch 2; keeping last loop of each st on hook, 2 dc in lst ch, yo and draw through all 3 loops on hook, pull tight; rep from * to **. End off. Sew to nose, tucking beginning slip knot behind center cluster.

Wheels

Make 2. Ch 2; 8 sc in lst ch, join, ch 1; working in back lps only, 1 sc in each sc, join. End off, leaving 8 inches yarn for sewing. Thread yarn in to needle, weave in and out of 8 sc just made, draw up tightly without distorting round shape. Sew top half of each wheel 3 sc below and in line with front edge of wing.

Christmas basket

This project is perfect for your holiday centerpiece. Sally George suggests filling it with cookies, apples, pinecones or Christmas cards. Or you might fill it with small gifts to take along for party favors.

If you're in a hurry or just want a small project, make the holly berry leaves alone and attach them to packages or turn them into lapel pins. Aren't these great stocking stuffers or inexpensive bazaar projects?

Materials: Acrylic 4-ply knitting worsted weight yarn—2 oz. off-white, ½ oz. each of red and medium green yarn, several yards of emerald green; 7 yards braided cotton clothesline or sash cord (³/₁₆-inch diameter, #6); masking or transparent tape; white thread.
Hook: #F and #G

Directions

No gauge is given, since it will differ with each type of filler cord used. The basket is approximately 9 inches high with handle, 3½ inches without. The bottom of the basket is about 6¼ inches in diameter, and the top is approximately 8 inches in diameter.

Basket

Bottom
Beginning at center with off-white and F hook, ch 3, join to form ring.
Rnd 1: Ch 1, 8 sc into ring. Do not join with sl st but work in continuous spiral, marking beg of each rnd with strand of contrasting-color yarn carried up each rnd.

Cut blunt end of clothesline to a taper. (Do not cut off a premeasured length of line but let it feed from the package.) Place clothesline on top of sts of rnd 1 and work all sts in all following rnds over it.
Rnd 2: (2 sc in each of next 3 sc, 3 sc in next sc) twice (18 sc).
Rnd 3: 2 sc in each sc (36 sc).
Rnd 4: (2 sc in next sc, 1 sc in each of next 2 sc) 12 times (48 sc).
Rnd 5: (1 sc in each of next 3 sc, 2 sc in next sc) 12 times (60 sc).
Rnd 6: (1 sc in each of next 4 sc, 2 sc in next sc) 12 times (72 sc).
Rnd 7: (1 sc in each of next 5 sc, 2 sc in next sc) 12 times (84 sc).

Rnd 8: (1 sc in each of next 6 sc, 2 sc in next sc) 12 times (96 sc).

Side
Rnd 9: Holding clothesline behind sc of previous rnd and working in back lps only, (1 sc in each of next 6 sc, dec next 2 sc) 12 times (84 sc). Pull gently on line as you work, drawing up scs to keep this rnd same circumference as previous rnd and to make nice sharp edge where side begins.
Rnd 10: Holding line on top of sc, (1 sc in each of next 6 sc, 2 sc in next sc) 12 times (96 sc). Although this is an increase in sts, do not allow basket to flare at this time. Additional sts are needed to cover clothesline—so pull line as you work to keep this rnd same size as previous rnds.
Rnd 11: 1 sc in each sc (96 sc). Keep line same size as rnd 10.
Rnd 12: (2 sc in next sc, 1 sc in each of next 7 sc) 12 times (108 sc). Now you can allow a little more line in rnd to create a slight flare.
Next 2 rnds: 1 sc in each sc (108 sc). At the end of rnd 14, work off the last lp of the last sc with medium green. Drop off-white but do not cut.
Rnd 15: Continuing with green, 1 sc in each sc, working off last lp of last sc with red. End off green.
Rnd 16: Continuing with red, 1 sc in each sc to within last 10 sc. At this point, cut clothesline, on a taper, where it will end rnd. Untwist a strand of 4-ply red yarn to get a strand of 2-ply. Thread this into a sharp needle and sew tapered end of clothesline to previous rnd, taking a few stitches through clothesline, then whipping over it to prevent fraying. Again with red 4-ply, sc in each of remaining sc, working off last lp of last sc with off-white. End off red.
Rnd 17: Continuing with off-white, 1 sc in next sc, ch 1, do not turn, but work reverse sc around, join to 1st reverse sc. End off off-white.

Handle: Measure and cut off 40 inches of clothesline. Place cut ends together, forming a large circle. With sewing thread or 2-ply yarn thread into sharp needle, take long stitches from one end to other. To hide frayed ends, wrap seam tightly with tape.

With off-white and F hook, beginning any place on circle, 1 sc around circle, working sts closely together until line is completely covered, join. End off. Untwist a length of off-white to get 2-ply stands. Thread 1 strand into blunt-nosed yarn needle. Flatten circle. Working along underside, lace scs on two cords together for about 8 inches along middle, leaving 2 lps of equal size at each end. Place lps on opposite sides of basket, lining up one lp along ends of rnds to camouflage break in colors. Bottoms of lps should touch top of rnd 12. Sew securely in place.

Holly berries: Make 6. With red and G hook, ch 2, 8 sc in lst ch, join. Cut yarn, leaving a 6-inch tail. Weave tail through back lps of all 8 sc; pull up tight so wrong side of sc are showing. Tie 3 berries together in a group and set aside.

Holly leaves: Make 6—two in medium green and four in emerald green. With G hook ch 11, sl st in 10th ch, 1 sc in each of next 2 ch, 1 dc in next ch, ch 2, sl st in 2nd-last ch, 1 dc in next ch, 1 sc in next ch, 1 hdc in next ch, ch 2, sl st in 2nd-last ch, 1 hdc in next ch, 1 sc in next ch, 1 sc in next ch, sl st in next ch, ch 2, sl st in 2nd-last ch; lay tail of yarn along ch; working along opposite side of ch, sl st in next ch, 1 sc in next ch, 1 hdc in next ch, ch 2, sl st in 2nd-last ch, 1 hdc in next ch, 1 sc in next ch, 1 dc in next ch, ch 2, sl st in 2nd-last ch, 1 dc in next ch, sc in next ch, sl st in last 2 ch, join with sl st. End off, leaving 6 inches yarn.

Assembly: Sew 1 emerald green leaf on each branch of handle with tops meeting at fork. Sew tops of each medium green leaf above fork. Sew one cluster of 3 berries at top of last leaf.

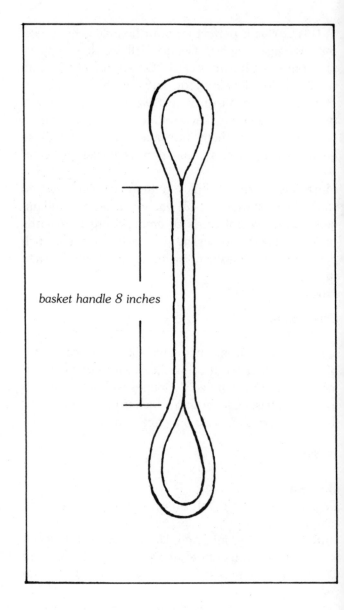

basket handle 8 inches

Three mouseketeers

What is better than one wee mouse hanging for dear life from a leaf? Three mice on a leaf! One of these projects makes an adorable hanging decoration. If you make all three, you can combine them into a mobile. The leaves are made in autumn colors, and the mice are gray—but you might like to make white ones.

Materials: Acrylic 4-ply knitting worsted weight yarn—several yards gray for mouse, several yards autumn color such as rust or brown for leaf, small amount of stuffing.

Hooks: #F for mouse
#G for leaf

Directions

The mouse is approximately 3 inches tall, the leaf is about 7 inches including stem.

Mouse

Head and body: Beginning at top of head, with gray, ch 2.

Rnd 1: 8 sc in lst ch. Do not join with a sl st but work in a continuous spiral, marking beginning of each rnd with strand of contrasting-color yarn which you carry up each rnd.

Rnd 2: (2 sc in next sc, 1 sc in next sc) 4 times (12 sc).

Next 2 rnds: 1 sc in each sc (12 sc).

Rnd 5: (Dec next 2 sc, 1 sc in next sc) 4 times (8 sc). Loop a short length of contrasting-color yarn under 3rd dec on rnd. This marks center front, where nose will be placed. Stuff head.

Rnd 6: (Dec next 2 sc, 1 sc in each of next 2 sc) twice (6 sc).

Rnd 7: (2 sc in next sc, 1 sc in next sc) 3 times (9 sc).

Rnd 8: 1 sc in each of next 3 sc, (2 sc in next sc, 1 sc in next sc) 3 times (12 sc).

Rnd 9: 1 sc in next sc, (2 sc in next sc, 1 sc in each of next 2 sc) 3 times, 2 sc in next sc, 1 sc in last sc (16 sc).

Rnd 10: 1 sc in each of next 5 sc, (2 sc in next sc, 1 sc in each of next 3 sc) twice, 2 sc in next sc, 1 sc in each of next 2 sc (19 sc).

Rnd 11: 1 sc in each of next 5 sc, 2 sc in next sc, 1 sc in each of next 10 sc, 2 sc in next sc, 1 sc in each of next 2 sc (21 sc).

Rnd 12: 1 sc in each sc (21 sc).

Rnd 13: 1 sc in each of next 5 sc, (dec next 2 sc, 1 sc in each of next 2 sc) 4 times (17 sc).

Rnd 14: (dec next 2 sc, 1 sc in next sc) 5 times, dec next 2 sc (11 sc). Stuff body.

Rnd 15: (Dec next 2 sc) 5 times, 1 sc in last sc (6 sc). End off, leaving 4 inches yarn; weave through remaining sts to close up.

Nose: With 4-ply gray yarn in needle, whipstitch in place over and over around the decreased scs that you marked at center front of head. Build up a small ball of sts (to make snout) until size suits your fancy.

Split a strand of black 4-ply to get a length of 2-ply. Use that to take a few tiny stitches on tip of ball for tiny black nose.

Eyes: Using the black 2-ply yarn, satin stitch small dots on rnd 4 of head, on either side of nose.

Left leg: With gray, ch 2.

Rnd 1: 6 sc in lst ch. Do not join; mark rnds as before.

Rnd 2: 2 sc in each sc (12 sc).

Rnd 3: Ch 6, sc in 2nd-last ch, sl st in each of next 4 ch, making leg; l sc in next sc, sl st in back lps of each of next 3 sc, 1 sc (under both lps again) in each of next 6 sc, sl st in back lps of each of next 2 sc; passing hook behind leg, join with sl st to lst sc. End off, leaving 6 inches yarn for sewing.

Right leg: Make the same as for left leg through rnd 2.

Rnd 3: Ch 6, sc in 2nd-last ch, sl st in each of next 4 ch, making leg; sl st in back lps of each of next 2 sc, 1 sc (under both lps) of each of next 6 sc, sl st in back lps of each of next 3 sc, 1 sc in next sc, join at base of ch that forms leg. End off, leaving 6 inches yarn for sewing.

Put small amount of stuffing in each haunch. Place on sides of body over rnds 11 to 13. Sew securely.

Ears: Make 2. With gray, ch 2.

Rnd 1: 7 sc in lst ch. Do not join; mark rnds.

Rnd 2: (2 sc in next sc, 1 sc in next sc) 3 times, 2 sc in last sc, sl st in next sc (11 sc). End off, leaving 4 inches yarn for sewing. Sew to sides of head along rnds 2 and 3.

Arms: Make 2. Insert hook under an sc on rnd 8 at side of body; draw up lp, ch 11, 1 sc in 2nd-last ch, sl st in each remaining ch. End off, securely weaving both tails of yarn into body.

Tail: Insert hook under an sc on rnd 14 at center back; draw up a lp, ch 24. Cut yarn, leaving 2 inches, weave about 1 inch back through end of ch, trimming off excess. Grasp tip of tail and twist into spiral; pull tight and release—it will spring into a curl! (Honest.)

One last finishing touch . . . with yarn in needle, take a few stitches from chest to chin, drawing head down so nose touches tummy.

Oak leaf

Beginning with the stem, with color of choice and G hook, ch 7, sc in 2nd-last ch and each of next 4 ch (leaving one ch unworked) (5 sc).

Row 1: Ch 7, sc in 2nd-last ch and each of next 5 ch, sk end of stem, 1 sc in unworked beginning ch, ch 6, turn (7 sc).

Row 2: Sc in 2nd-last ch and each of next 4 ch, sk next sc, 1 sc in each of next 5 sc, 2 sc in last sc, ch 1, turn (12 sc).

Row 3: 2 sc in lst sc, 1 sc in each of next 5 sc, sk next sc, 1 sc in each of next 4 sc, 2 sc in last sc, ch 1, turn (13 sc).

Row 4: 2 sc in lst sc, sc in each of next 4 sc, sk next sc, 1 sc in each of next 4 sc, ch 7, turn (10 sc).

Row 5: 1 sc in 2nd-last ch and each of next 5 ch, 1 sc in each of next 3 sc, sk next sc, 1 sc in each of next 3 sc, ch 7, turn (12 sc).

Row 6: 1 sc in 2nd ch from hook and each of next 5 ch, 1 sc in each of next 3 sc, sk next sc, 1 sc in each of next 7 sc, 2 sc in last sc, ch 1, turn (18 sc).

Row 7: 2 sc in lst sc, 1 sc in each of next 8 sc, sk next sc, 1 sc in each of next 7 sc, 2 sc in last sc, ch 1, turn (19 sc).

Row 8: 2 sc in lst sc, 1 sc in each of next 8 sc, sk next sc, 1 sc in each of next 5 sc, ch 5, turn (15 sc).

Row 9: 1 sc in 2nd-last ch and each of next 3 ch, 1 sc in each of next 5 sc, sk next sc, 1 sc in each of next 5 sc, ch 5, turn (14 sc).

Row 10: 1 sc in 2nd-last ch and each of next 3 ch, 1 sc in each of next 5 sc, sk next sc, 1 sc in each of next 7 sc, 2 sc in last sc, ch 1, turn (18 sc).

Row 11: 2 sc in lst sc, 1 sc in each of next 8 sc, sk next sc, 1 sc in each of next 7 sc, 2 sc in last sc, ch 1, turn (19 sc).

Row 12: 2 sc in first sc, 1 sc in each of next 8 sc, sk next sc, 1 sc in each of next 4 sc, ch 5, turn (14 sc).

Row 13: 1 sc in 2nd-last ch and each of next 3 ch, 1 sc in each of next 4 sc, sk next sc, 1 sc in each of next 4 sc, ch 4, turn (12 sc).

Row 14: 1 sc in 2nd-last ch and each of next 2 ch, 1 sc in each of next 4 sc, sk next sc, 1 sc in each of next 6 sc, 2 sc in last sc, ch 1, turn (15 sc).

Row 15: 2 sc in lst sc, 1 sc in each of next 6 sc, sk next 2 sc, 1 sc in each of next 5 sc, 2 sc in last sc, ch 1, turn (15 sc).

Row 16: 2 sc in lst sc, 1 sc in each of next 5 sc, sk next 2 sc, 1 sc in each of next 2 sc, ch 4, turn (9 sc).

Row 17: (Center point of leaf) 1 sc in 2nd-last ch and each of next 2 ch, sk next sc, sl st in each of next 2 sc, turn (5 sc).

Row 18: Pull yarn across front of sl sts to back, sk one sl st, 1 sc in next sl st, 1 sc in each of next 2 sc, 2 sc in last sc, ch 1, turn (5 sc).

Row 19: 1 sc in each of next 5 sc, sl st in next sc (6th sc made in row 16). Cut yarn and pull tail through sl st (not lp on hook). Weave tail into center of leaf.

Assembly: Sew mouse to leaf in one of the poses shown in the photo. Use a strand of gray 4-ply yarn split into 2-ply. If you take short whipstitches from end of arm over edge of leaf, sts will look like tiny mouse fingers. Attach a hanging thread of yarn, thread or monofilament cut to desired length.

Hang over breakfast table, kitchen sink, in any window, over crib, playpen or car seat, or among your hanging plants.

To make a mobile, add a half dozen more leaves in assorted colors hung at assorted heights.

Iris candleholder and candle

This candleholder and candle decoration are designed to look like an iris. Sally George says that she made it with purple yarn because that's what she associates with an iris. Actually, her garden yields all colors, so she suggests that you use your imagination. This might be just the thing for a Christmas window display to replace the real thing.

Materials: Acrylic 4-ply knitting worsted weight yarn—1 oz. Main Color (MC) for flower, ½ oz. yellow (or white) for beard, ½ oz. color of choice for candle (lavender used here), a few yards yellow for candle flame; cocktail toothpicks or plastic pins from hair rollers; cardboard tube (toilet paper or paper towels).
Hook: #G
Gauge: 4 sc = 1 inch
4 rows sc = 1 inch

Directions

The iris is 4 inches high and 6 inches across. The candle can be any height desired. This one is approximately 6½ inches high.

Candle holder

Cup: Starting at center of bottom, with MC, ch 2.
Rnd 1: 8 sc in lst ch, join, ch 1.
Rnd 2: 2 sc in each sc, join, ch 1 (16 sc).
Rnd 3: (1 sc in next sc, 2 sc in next sc) 8 times, join, ch 1, turn (24 sc).
Rnd 4: Working in back lps only, 1 sc in sl st, 1 sc in each of next 23 sc, join, ch 1 (24 sc).
Next 6 Rnds: 1 sc in each sc, join, ch 1. End off.

Lower petals: Make 3. Starting at center, with yellow, ch 6.
Rnd 1: 1 sc in 2nd-last ch, 2 sc in each of next 2 ch, sc in next ch, 4 sc in end ch; working along opposite side of ch, lay beg tail of yarn on top of ch and work following sts over it: 1 sc in next ch, 2 sc in each of next 2 ch, 1 sc in last ch, turn (16 sc). End off yellow.
Rnd 2: Working in front lps only, attach MC in first sc, ch 1, 1 sc in same sc, 1 sc in next sc, work 2 decreases in next 4 sc, 2 dc in next sc, (1 dc, 3 tr) in next sc, (3 tr, 1 dc) in next sc, 2 dc in next sc; working in sc, make 2 decs in next 4 sc, 1 sc in each of next 2 sc, ch 1 (20 sts). Rotate piece so end of yellow strip is

at top.
Rnd 3: Working across top of yellow strip, sl st in same st with last sc, sl st into beg ch at center of yellow strip between 2 yellow sc, sl st into first MC sc, ch 1; rotate piece so beg of rnd 2 is at top; sl st in first sc, sk next sc, sl st in next sc, sk next sc, 2 sc in dc, 1 sc in next dc, 2 dc in next dc, 2 dc in each of next 2 tr, (1 dc, 2 tr) in next tr, (2 tr, 1 dc) in next tr, 2 dc in each of next 2 tr, 2 dc in next dc, 1 sc in next dc, 2 sc in next dc, sk next sc, sl st in next sc, sk next sc, sl st in last sc, sl st in ch 1. End off, leaving 5 inches for sewing.

Upper petals: Make 3. Starting at center with MC, ch 10.
Rnd 1: 1 sc in 2nd-last ch and each of next 7 ch; 4 sc in end ch; working along opposite side of ch, lay beg tail of yarn on top of ch and work following sts over it: 1 sc in each of next 8 ch, ch 1, turn (16 sc).
Rnd 2: Working in front lps only, 1 sc in each of next 6 sc, dec next 2 sc, 2 dc in next sc, (1 dc, 3 tr) in next sc, (3 tr, 1 dc) in next sc, 2 dc in next sc; working in sc, make 1 dec in next 2 sc, 1 sc in each of next 6 sc, ch 1 (26 sts).
Rnd 3: Rotate piece so narrow end is at top; sl st in same st with last sc, sl st into beg ch at center of piece, sl st at bottom of sc of rnd 2, sl st in top of same sc, ch 1; rotate piece so beg of rnd 2 is at top; 1 sc in first sc and each of next 5 sc, sk next sc, 2 sc in dc, 1 sc in next dc, 2 dc in next dc, 2 dc in next tr, (1 dc, 1 tr) in next tr, (1 tr, 1 dc) in next tr, (1 dc, 1 tr) in next tr, (1 tr, 1 dc) in next tr, 2 dc in tr, 2 dc in dc, 1 sc in next dc, 2 sc in dc, sk next sc, 1 sc in each of next 6 sc, sl st in ch 1. End off, leaving 10 inches yarn for sewing.

Assembly:
Place flat edge of one of lower petals along top edge of cup so beard curves outward. Sew in place, taking needle through the top lps only on petal and both lps on edge of cup. Sew other 2 lower petals, equally spaced, onto cup. Arrange 3 upper petals between lower petals with their flat edges lined up with bottom edge of cup. Pin in place with toothpicks or curler pins. Sew along bottom edge and up each side. You may have to pinch them a bit to make them fit in between other petals. Take a few invisible sts on inside of petal to hold it to top edge of cup.

Candle

These candles, with their clever little drips of wax, are made separately from the candle holders so they can be slipped off and washed or folded flat for storage.

The directions make a crocheted candle that will fit over cardboard tubes from toilet paper, paper towels, plastic wrap, gift wrap or aluminum foil.

You can make any height candle you want by cutting down the longer tubes or taping 2 shorter tubes together.

All tubes vary in circumference. If yours measures 5 inches around, it is of smaller variety, so make your beginning ch 21 sts instead of 23. It will still fit candle holder.

Decide upon height of your candle before crocheting. Crochet cover ¼ inch shorter than cardboard tube—bare tube seems to fit better into bottom of cup.

Candle tube: Starting at bottom, ch 23 (21), 1 sc into lst ch to form ring.

Rnd 1: 1 sc in each ch. Do not join with a sl st but work in a continuous spiral, marking beg of each rnd with a strand of contrasting-color yarn carried up each rnd.

Continue 1 sc in each sc to height desired.

Next Rnd: 1 sc in each of next 15 sc, ch 1, turn.

Next Rnd: Sk first sc, 1 sc in each of next 12 (10) sc, sl st in each of next 2 sc, ch 10 to begin first drip, * 3 sc in 2nd-last ch, sl st in each remaining ch, sl st in same sc with beg of ch **, sl st in next sc, ch 8 to begin 2nd drip, repeat directions from * to **, sl st in each of next 6 sc, ch 12 to begin 3rd drip, repeat directions from * to **, sl st in next sc, sl st into ch 1. End off.

Untwist a 4-ply strand of matching yarn to get two 2-ply strands. Use these strands to sew each drip to side of candle.

Sally suggests, "Each time you make a candle, make the drips different lengths. Not that anyone will think these are real candles, but its fun to add variety to the illusion."

Flame: With yellow or gold, ch 6, 2 sc in 2nd-last ch, 1 hdc in next ch, 1 dc in next ch, 1 sc in next ch, sl st in next ch, ch 2, sl st in 2nd-last ch; working along opposite side of ch, lay beg tail of yarn on top of ch and work following sts over it: sl st in lst ch, 1 sc in next ch, 1 hdc in next ch, 2 dc in next ch, 1 sc in last ch, sl st to join. End off, leaving 4 inches yarn for sewing. Set aside.

Candle top: Beginning at center, with yarn matching candle, ch 2.

Rnd 1: 7 sc in lst ch. Do not join—mark rnds.

Rnd 2: 2 sc in each sc around (14 sc).

Rnd 3: (1 sc in next sc, 2 sc in next sc) 7 times (21 sc). End off, leaving 8 inches yarn for sewing.

Assembly: Place flame in center of candle top and sew in place. Place candle top inside rim of candle tube. Sew in place, taking needle under both lps of sc on top but under only one—the inner—lp of sc on tube. Cut a slanted piece off one end of cardboard tube. Slip cardboard tube, slanted edge first, into crocheted tube, lining up high edges. Slip candle into holder of your choice. You will have to stretch cup on holder to fit over fatter candles.

Mouse yarnimal

This and the following projects were designed by Anne Lane of North Abington, Massachusetts. She has generously shared her patterns for these delightful quick and easy bazaar and gift ideas. You can see more of her patterns by writing to her. (See source list at end of book.)

This little mouse measures approximately 11 inches high and would make an equally good gift for a baby and a teenager. The pink flared dress is even removable. What fun for the child who receives this toy!

Materials: Knitting worsted—1 oz. gray, 1 oz. hot pink; 2 small buttons or black embroidery floss for eyes; white carpet thread for whiskers and for sewing eyes in place; small amount of pink floss; small scraps of pink felt for ear linings; polyfil stuffing for head, body, arms, legs and nose.
Hook: Size #00

Directions

Head and body

Starting at top of head, with gray yarn ch 2.
Rnd 1: 6 sc in lst ch. Do not join rnds; carry piece of contrasting-color yarn between lst and last sc to mark beg of rnds.
Rnd 2: Inc in each sc around (12 sc).
Rnd 3: * 1 sc in lst sc, inc in next sc. Rep from * around (18 sc).
Rnd 4: * 1 sc in each of lst 2 sc, inc in next sc. Rep from * around (24 sc).
Rnds 5–9: Work even on 24 sc.
Rnd 10: * 1 sc in each of lst 2 sc, dec over next 2 sc. Rep from * around (18 sc).
Rnd 11: * 1 sc in first sc, dec over next 2 sc. Rep from * around (12 sc). Stuff head firmly before opening becomes too small.
Rnd 12: Dec 6 sc evenly spaced around (6 sc).
Rnd 13: Work even on 6 sc.
Rnd 14: Inc in each sc around (12 sc).
Rnd 15: * 1 sc in lst sc, inc in next sc. Rep from * around (18 sc).
Rnd 16: * 1 sc in each of lst 2 sc, inc in next sc. Rep from * around (24 sc).
Rnds 17–21: Work even on 24 sc. At end of rnd 21 end off gray yarn and join pink yarn.
Rnds 22–27: Work even on 24 sc. End off at end of rnd 27, leaving a 12-inch length of yarn for sewing.

Legs

Make 2. Starting at top of leg, with pink yarn, ch 12. Join with sl st.
Rnd 1: 1 sc in each ch around (12 sc), being careful not to twist ch. Do not join rnds; mark as for head and body.
Rnd 2: Repeat rnd 1. At end of rnd 2 end off pink yarn and join gray yarn.
Rnds 3–9: Work even on 12 sc.
Rnd 10: * 1 sc in each of lst 2 sc, dec over next 2 sc. Rep from * around (9 sc).
Rnd 11: Work even on 9 sc.
Rnd 12: * 1 sc in each of lst 2 sc, inc in next sc. Rep from * around (12 sc).
Rnds 13 and 14: Work even on 12 sc. End off at end of rnd 14.

Soles

Make 2. With gray yarn, ch 2.
Rnd 1: 6 sc in lst ch. Do not join rnds—mark as for head and body.
Rnd 2: Inc in each sc around (12 sc). End off, leaving an 8-inch length of yarn for sewing sole to leg.

Arms

Make 2. Starting at tip of arm, with gray yarn, ch 2.
Rnd 1: 6 sc in lst ch. Do not join rnds—mark as for head and body.
Rnd 2: Inc in first sc, 1 sc in each remaining sc (7 sc).
Rnd 3: 1 sc in each of lst 3 sc, inc in next sc, 1 sc in each of last 3 sc (8 sc).
Rnd 4: 1 sc in each of lst 7 sc, inc in last sc (9 sc).
Rnds 5–12: Work even on 9 sc. End off at end of rnd 12, leaving a 12-inch length of yarn for sewing.

Ears

Make 2. With gray yarn, ch 2.
Row 1: 5 sc in lst ch. Ch 1 and turn.
Row 2: Inc in each sc across (10 sc). Ch 1 and turn.
Row 3: 1 sc in each of lst 3 sc, inc in each of next 3 sc, 1 sc in each of last 4 sc (13 sc). End off, leaving 6-inch length for sewing ear to head.

Nose

Starting at tip of nose, with gray yarn, ch 2.

Rnd 1: 6 sc in lst ch. Do not join rnds—mark as for head and body.

Rnd 2: Work even on 6 sc.

Rnd 3: * 1 sc in lst sc, inc in next sc. Rep from * around (9 sc).

Rnd 4: * 1 sc in each of lst 2 sc, inc in next sc. Rep from * around (12 sc).

End off, leaving a 12-inch length of yarn for sewing nose to head.

Finish: Finish stuffing head and body very firmly and sew across rnd 27. Stuff both arms very firmly and sew across rnd 12 of each arm. Sew arms to body at shoulders.

Next sew a sole to bottom of each leg, then stuff both legs firmly and sew across rnd 1 of each leg. Sew legs securely at bottom of body.

Stuff nose firmly and sew it to head, centering it on lower part. From scraps of pink felt cut ear linings, making them slightly smaller than ears themselves. Sew linings to insides of ears with pink thread, using a neat overcast stitch. Sew ears to head near top.

Using white carpet thread, sew eyes firmly to head just above nose—or with black embroidery floss make 2 French knots for eyes. Use pink embroidery floss to make several vertical stitches at tip of nose.

Run a doubled strand of white carpet thread through the nose several times about 2 sc back from tip of nose. Trim to desired length for whiskers.

Dress

Skirt: Using pink yarn, ch 32 loosely.

Rnd 1: 1 dc in 3rd-last ch and in each of remaining 29 ch (30 dc). Join with a sl st.

Rnd 2: Ch 3 (to count as a dc), 1 dc in joining st, 2 dc in each dc around (60 dc), join to top of ch 3 with a sl st.

Rnd 3: Ch 3 (to count as a dc), 3 dc in joining st, 4 dc in each dc around. Join to top of ch 3 with a sl st. End off.

Bodice: Join yarn to opposite side of the starting ch.

Row 1: Ch 3 (to count as a dc), 1 dc in each of remaining 29 ch (30 dc). Ch 3 and turn (to count as lst dc of next row).

Row 2: Work even on 30 dc. Ch 3 and turn (to count as first dc of next row).

Row 3: 1 dc in each of lst 5 dc, ch 4, skip 4 dc (this forms an armhole), 1 dc in each of next 3 dc, ch 4, skip 4 dc (this forms other armhole), 1 dc in each of remaining 6 dc. Ch 25 for lst back tie. End off. Join yarn to other end of this row and ch 25. End off.

This wonderful crib toy can sit quietly in a corner or hang as a mobile. If you put him on an elastic to hang, he will bounce up and down when given a slight tug. Anne Lane's clown is made with red and white yarns, but this might be a good time to let your imagination run wild. Combine all the colorful scraps in your yarn basket and make each one differently.

Materials: Knitting worsted—1 oz. red, ½ oz. pink, ½ oz. white; red and black embroidery floss; polyfil stuffing.

Hooks: #H and #00

Directions

Arms and legs
Make 2. With red and H hook, ch 82.
Rnd 1: 2 dc in 3rd-last ch, 3 dc in each remaining ch. End off.

Head
With pink and 00 hook, ch 2.
Rnd 1: 6 sc in 2nd-last ch. Do not join rnds—carry a piece of contrasting-color yarn between first and last sc to mark beg of rnds.
Rnd 2: Inc in each sc around (12 sc).
Rnds 3–5: Working in sc, inc 6 sc evenly spaced in each rnd (30 sc on rnd 5).
Rnds 6–11: Work even on 30 sc.
Rnds 12–14: Continuing to work in sc, dec 6 sc evenly spaced in each rnd (12 sc on rnd 14). Stuff head firmly before opening becomes too small.
Rnd 15: Dec 6 sc evenly spaced around (6 sc). End off, leaving a 12-inch length of yarn for sewing.

Body half
Make 2. With red and H hook, ch 11.
Row 1: 1 sc in 2nd-last ch and in each remaining ch (10 sc). Ch 1 and turn.
Rows 2–12: Work even on 10 sc. Ch 1 and turn at end of each row. End off at end of row 12.

Neck ruffle
With white yarn and H hook, ch 15.
Rnd 1: 2 dc in 3rd-last ch, 3 dc in each remaining ch. End off, leaving 12-inch length of yarn for sewing.

Hat
With red and 00 hook, ch 2.
Rnd 1: 6 sc in 2nd-last ch. Do not join rnds—mark as for head.
Rnd 2 and all even-numberd rnds: Work even on number of sc in previous rnd.
Rnd 3: Inc in each sc around (12 sc).
Rnd 5: * 1 sc in lst sc, inc in next sc. Rep from * around (18 sc).
Rnd 7: * 1 sc in each of lst 2 sc, inc in next sc. Rep from * around (24 sc).
Rnd 9: * 1 sc in each of lst 3 sc, inc in next sc. Rep from * around (30 sc).
Rnd 10: Work even on 30 sc. End off red yarn and join white yarn.
Rnd 11: (Work in back lps only) 3 dc in each sc around, join with sl st. End off, leaving 12-inch length of yarn for sewing.

Finish
Twist arms and legs spirals until curled and sew together at 8th spiral. These first 8 spirals form arms, the longer spirals are legs.

Sew head firmly to arms and legs at joining point. Next sew body half pieces together with several overcast stitches at middle of bottom edges. Slip over legs and up to neck. Sew shoulder seams. Sew side seams from bottom to underarms.

Place neck ruffle around neck. Sew ends together and sew neck ruffle to bottom of head. Sew hat to top of head.

With black embroidery floss, make 2 crossed stitches for eyes. With red embroidery floss, embroider a nose and a smiling mouth.

If you want a jingly clown, Anne Lane suggests adding small bells to ends of arms and legs.

Ladybug change purse

Anne Lane's ladybug with the movable eyes has a loop handle for carrying, and the best feature is the snap-open head. Little children will love carrying their change inside the body, and can also hang it from a belt for safe keeping. Our four-year-old model (page 159) could hardly put it down long enough for us to photograph it.

Materials: Knitting worsted—¼ oz. red, ¼ oz. black; 1 large snap; 2 movable eyes; carpet thread; red embroidery floss for mouth.
Hook: #00

Directions

Top of body
   With red, ch 2.
Rnd 1: 6 sc in lst ch. Do not join rnds—carry a piece of contrasting-color yarn between first and last sc to mark beg of rnds.
Rnd 2: Inc in each sc around (12 sc).
Rnds 3—6: Working in sc, inc 6 sc evenly spaced in each rnd (36 sc on rnd 6).
Rnds 7—8: Work even on 36 sc. At end of rnd 8 end off red yarn and join black yarn.
Rnd 9: Work even on 36 sc. End off, leaving 14-inch length of yarn for sewing.

Bottom of body
   With black, ch 2.
Rnd 1: 8 sc in lst ch. Do not jn rnds—mark as for top of body.
Rnd 2: Inc in each sc around (16 sc).
Rnds 3—6: Working in sc, inc 8 sc evenly spaced in each rnd (48 sc in rnd 6). End off.

Head
   With black, ch 2.
Row 1: Make 5 sc in lst ch. Ch 1 and turn.
Row 2: Inc in each sc (10 sc). Ch 1 and turn.
Row 3: * 1 sc in lst sc, inc in next sc. Rep from * four times (15 sc). Ch 1 and turn.
Row 4: * 1 sc in each of lst 2 sc, inc in next sc. Repeat from * four times (20 sc). End off.

Antenna: Make 2. With black, ch 6.
Row 1: 1 sc in 2nd-last ch and in each of next 4 ch. End off.

Spots: Make 5. With black, ch 2.
Rnd 1: 6 sc in 2nd-last ch. Join with sl st; end off.

Note: If you prefer, the spots can be made from ½-inch circles of black felt and glued on with craft glue.

Belt loop or strap
　With black, ch 4.
Row 1: 1 sc in 2nd-last ch and in each of next 2 ch. Ch 1 and turn. Work even in sc for 4 inches or desired length. End off.

Finish: Sew top of body to bottom of body using neat overcast sts. Leave 10 sc not sewn tog. These will form opening of purse.

　Using black yarn sew straight edge of head to back lps of bottom of body at opening. Sew wiggle eyes on head. Sew one half of snap to head and the other half to top of body. Sew spots to top of body.

　Double belt loop or strap and sew ends tog. Attach firmly to bottom of body. Sew mouth with red floss.

ladybug snaps open to make minipurse

Source list

If you have trouble obtaining any of the yarns specified for the projects, you can write to the following addresses for information on mail-order sources or for the name of a store in your area that carries the material.

Bernat Yarn and Craft Corp.
Uxbridge, Massachusetts 01569

Bucilla Yarns
150 Meadowland Parkway
Secaucus, New Jersey 07094

Coats & Clark
75 Rockefeller Plaza
New York, New York 10019

Gemini innovations ltd. (ribbons)
720 East Jericho Turnpike
Huntington Station, New York 11746

Laines Anny Blatt
Applegate Square
29775 Northwestern Highway
Southfield, Michigan 48034

Phildar, Inc.
6438 Dawson Boulevard
Norcross, Georgia 30093

Tahki Imports Ltd.
92 Kennedy Street
Hackensack, New Jersey 07601

Mail order for Phildar yarns

Creative Needles
436 Avenue of the Americas
New York, New York 10011

Mail order for crochet patterns

Anne Lane Originals
P.O. Box 206
North Abington, Massachusetts 02351

Sally V. George
The Crochet Works
1472 Auburn
Baker, Oregon 97814
(catalog 50¢)

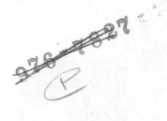